David Brown was born in Nottingham but moved to Bath in 1980 and has lived in the West Country ever since. He studied Business Administration at Bath University before working first in marketing and then in retail, managing a fair trading shop in the city centre. Following encouragement from his minister David trained as a lay preacher in the Methodist Church and was recognized as such in 1984. Worship has always been important to him and he feels constantly challenged by the need to make it inspiring and relevant to twenty-first century people without alienating those already within the Church. Music has been a part of his life ever since childhood and he has produced and sung in a number of musicals at church and written the lyrics to a new one. He met his wife, Heather, an electronic engineer, at church and they were married in 1994. He has recently started a small travel business, taking people on days out from Bath and on customized holidays to Snowdonia. In his spare time he enjoys photography, narrow-gauge steam trains and rock music.

Coming to Life

Stories of God in the Everyday

David Brown

First published in Great Britain in 2003 by
Society for Promoting Christian Knowledge
Holy Trinity Church
Marylebone Road
London NW1 4DU

Scripture quotations taken from the
HOLY BIBLE, NEW INTERNATIONAL VERSION
copyright © 1973, 1978, 1984 by International Bible Society.
Used by permission of Hodder & Stoughton Ltd,
a member of the Hodder Headline Plc Group.

Extract from the Covenant Service of the Methodist Church is
copyright © Trustees for Methodist Church Purposes, and used
by permission of Methodist Publishing House.

British Library Cataloguing-in-Publication Data
A catalogue record for this book is available from the
British Library

ISBN 0-281-05563-7

1 3 5 7 9 10 8 6 4 2

Typeset by FiSH Books, London WC1
Printed in Great Britain by Bookmarque Ltd, Croydon, Surrey

Contents

For my wife, Heather,
who encouraged me and without whose support
this book would not have been possible

Introduction

I have always envied Moses. Not that I particularly crave forty years in the wilderness, nor do I fancy the responsibility that he carried. But I envy his closeness to God. Here was a man who did not have to struggle to see evidence of the Divine. It was all around him, from the burning bush to parted seas, in manna from the skies and on tablets of stone. The reality of God was all too evident, culminating in those occasions when Moses climbed the mountain to talk to him 'face to face', as it were. There was no room for doubt. God was clearly alive and at work and a living reality.

There have been others to envy too, not just biblical figures. As a teenager I went to hear Nicky Cruz speak in Nottingham (he of *The Cross and the Switchblade* fame), and I was left in awe of this man who so clearly saw God at work in the ghetto. He saw miracles happen and knew God to be real because of what he was doing in his own life and in the lives of those around him. It made an indelible impression on me. Later on at university I came across people who spoke in tongues and who clearly knew that God was present in their lives and again I envied their experience. Even as a grown man, approaching middle age, I could still be bowled over by the faith of our lay worker at church, a man whose entire family lived hand-to-mouth in the confident faith that God would provide. And they were never disappointed.

The trouble was, and is for that matter, that I have never seen an angel, never heard God speak to me, never been struck by the equivalent of a thunderbolt. I firmly believe in God, to the extent that I have been for some twenty years a preacher in the Methodist Church, but in all that time I have never felt a direct contact. If I look back I can see that God has clearly been at work in my life – shaping and moulding and directing me at all stages. But it has never been a dramatic kind of work and that used to worry me. Was my faith, my experience, somehow less real than that of other people? Was I some sort of 'second-class' Christian, just because I had never heard heavenly voices or seen a lame person walk? Then I began to talk to others and to share my concerns and I discovered that many on the journey of faith felt the same. We probably all have a saint of our own – someone whose faith leaves us breathless and inspired, but for most of us our own personal encounter with God is in the ordinary, everyday experiences of life, often visible only with hindsight, seen only from a distance.

There are many books about the people who inspire us, many books about faith and living with God's amazing presence. But I wanted to write in a slightly different way. I strongly believe that God performs most of his work in the humdrum of daily existence and so I set about writing a book that would examine real life through short stories, each of them offering different insights into biblical and theological truth. Admittedly on two occasions the stories took off in a somewhat less than ordinary direction but since they were written from a very personal viewpoint I felt they still qualified. As I wrote I found myself becoming fascinated with the *process* of truth, the ways in which people's lives become entangled with God and his Spirit and the manner in which they come to see the workings of God in their everyday experience. Thus I found myself painting pictures of very ordinary people encountering God in their own small ways in the hope that by so doing the reader would recognize something of his or her own experience in the characters and situations.

Each story that follows therefore says something about God and the way that our lives are, often unconsciously, bound up with him. After each story there is a short reflection to stimulate further thought, together with a biblical reference. The link may not always be obvious, yet in every case the Bible has been the source of truth that has inspired the story, the spring from which the flow of narrative has sprung, and one should always give credit where it is due. But there is also something here about the relevance of the Bible to our everyday lives. We may not live on manna and meet God on the mountaintops but each one of us is touched by the hand and the presence of God, even if that touch is somewhat subtle.

I hope these stories speak of that presence and that touch.

They, too, serve

Austin hated Wednesdays. Actually he wasn't overly fond of Tuesdays or Fridays, now you come to mention it. Nor were Mondays, Thursdays and Saturdays anything much to look forward to. But Sunday – now there was a day to be anticipated. Every Sunday Austin would get up and have a special bath and wash his hair using the special shampoo his granny always gave him for his birthday. He would dress in his brown suit and ask his long-suffering mother to tie his tie for him and he would eat his special Sunday breakfast. After that he would brush his teeth (two-and-a-half minutes, like the dentist said), and then he would take his long grey coat, whatever the weather, and walk the mile-and-a-bit to the church.

He was always early. Service wasn't until eleven, but when the stewards opened up the big old door they would usually find Austin waiting patiently in the porch.

'Hello!' he would always say, and they would smile, usually, and say hello in return and ask him what he wanted to do this morning. They always asked and he always said the same thing, 'Can I give out the hymn books, please?' And they would say that, yes, he could and he would clap his hands together and tell them that he liked giving out the books. He would go to the shelves where the books were all stored and start to sort them, ready to give to the people arriving for the service. Last year the church had held a Commitment Weekend, challenging its members to commit to something new in the life of the church. Austin wasn't sure what he could do but Gwendolyn had pointed out that people needed books and needed greeting and that she thought he would be good at doing that. And he was. Over time he had sorted out the shelves where the books were stored and had made sense of their wild jumble. Today he knew he needed the Service Book and *Mission Praise* because there was a christening and it was all-age worship. One from the top shelf and one from the special cupboard at the side. His system made it easy and soon he was ready for the people, ready and eager. This was why he looked forward to Sundays.

Lucy was not having a good time. She had been ready to go for twenty minutes now and still Wayne wasn't ready. Of course if he hadn't have come home last night quite so late or quite so drunk he wouldn't have slept through the alarm this morning and she wouldn't have come back upstairs after her breakfast to find him still asleep.

'We're going to be late!' she yelled up the stairs for the third or fourth time, 'and what will Brian and Melissa think of us then?' There was a sudden rush of footsteps on the staircase and Wayne came running down, half an arm in his jacket, hair still wet from the shower.

'What sort of godparents are late to their own godson's christening?' she shot at him as he ducked past her and out of the front door.

'Of all the nights to get drunk...' she accused as he fumbled with the car keys.

'I should never have agreed to you going out with Kevin last night,' as he burnt rubber on the road. They drove in manic silence for ten minutes, and then, 'I shall tell them there was an accident. We had to stop. Witnesses.'

Wayne just nodded his head. He knew when he was in trouble, and he knew when he deserved it. Today was such a day. Keep your head down, he thought, don't say anything, accept the blame, buy flowers tomorrow, everything would be OK by Wednesday. He hoped. Why did he have to mess up today of all days? Definitely flowers...and chocolates. OK by Thursday. Perhaps.

Austin was enjoying himself immensely. There were lots of extra people this morning for the christening and he was having to give out more books than he had ever given out before. And he didn't just give the books out. With every book he smiled and said 'hello' and told the person how pleased he was to see them this morning. He always played a kind of a game with himself. He lost if the person didn't smile at him in return, so if his 'hello' didn't produce a smile he always said something else. Sometimes it was the weather. That worked with certain people, but often he had found that a nice comment about their clothes or their hair or their suntan did the trick. He was getting quite good at finding the right compliment for the right person and he nearly always won his game. This morning was harder, though. He didn't know the christening people. Gwendolyn had told him they weren't church people at all, which had shocked him a bit, and he didn't know what to say to them if they didn't smile first time. He tried the weather and mostly got a polite response, but no smile. He tried clothes but gave up after a woman gave him a funny look when he said how nice her dress was. After that he didn't dare make comments about anyone's hair or face. Eventually he fell back on 'It's a pleasure to see you this morning,' which he had heard someone say once and thought sounded impressive and polite.

One woman, the mother of the baby, had come past him several times now. The first time he'd told her how lovely her son looked as she came into the church and she had flashed him the best smile of the morning. But she kept going back out again and each time she came back she looked less happy. He wasn't sure what to say the second time, so he just smiled but by the fourth time she looked so worried that he had to say something.

'Don't worry,' he said, 'the baby will be fine.' She just looked at him for a moment, and he wasn't sure what was in her face, but then she smiled. Not the best smile of the morning again, but a sad kind of a smile.

'I suppose he will,' she said. 'I just hoped Wayne was going to get something out of being a godparent, hoped he would take the responsibility seriously. He's a good man at heart. I thought it would do him good.' Austin just smiled his encouraging smile as her voice trailed off, and he nodded in what he thought was the right way. It must have been right, because the woman smiled again, a little brighter now. 'I'm sorry to burden you with my problems,' she said, 'but you're a very good listener.'

Austin wasn't sure what she meant but it sounded good so he smiled even more and said, 'You're welcome', like his mother had taught him.

His pleasure was short-lived, as the minister chose that moment to come up to Austin and the woman. 'Melissa,' he said, ignoring Austin completely, 'is there any sign of them yet?' Melissa shook her head. 'We can't wait much longer for them, I'm afraid,' the minister said and took the shaking of her head to mean that Melissa agreed with him. 'I'll start the service, then. They'll have about ten minutes before the christening ceremony itself,' and he bustled off down the aisle to the vestry. Austin never knew what to say to the minister. By all accounts the Reverend Watts was a very clever man and although Austin enjoyed his services he didn't actually understand very much of them. And they never seemed to know what to say to each other. To tell the truth, Austin quite often didn't know what to say, and here was another of those occasions as the woman, Melissa, looked down the path one last time and sighed before making her way down the aisle to her seat.

As the service began Austin took his seat at the back, right by the door. It wasn't really a proper seat but he liked to be close to the books in case anyone arrived late. He stood as everyone else did to sing the first hymn and was just about to settle down for the prayers when he saw two people come through the gate and start running up the path. For a moment he wondered what to do. Reverend Watts always said very long prayers and Austin knew better than to interrupt them by handing out books and making people smile. Usually people who were late crept in very quietly but these people didn't look very quiet so he got up and slipped through the door to meet them outside.

'Hello,' he said, as they came to a halt in front of him, and smiled his best smile. He was a bit disappointed when the woman didn't smile back but looked at him strangely.

'We're late,' she said, and gave the man an equally funny look. 'An accident. Have we missed anything?' Austin wasn't sure but he guessed that these were the people Melissa had been looking out for.

'Melissa will be very pleased to see you,' he said, 'but you can't go in just yet because Reverend Watts is saying his prayers and he likes to say them for a long time.' He leaned forward a little. 'I get a bit bored, sometimes,' he said, and was surprised but pleased to see the faintest flicker of a smile cross the woman's face.

'Are you Wayne?' he asked the man who was standing slightly behind the woman. The man looked up, surprise on his face.

'Yes,' he said. 'How did you know?' Austin put on what he thought of as his 'serious' face.

'Melissa thinks you are a good man,' he said solemnly, 'and she's hoping you will get something out of being a godfather.' The man looked startled, then slowly smiled at Austin, who smiled back, his game won. A sudden chorus of 'Amens' signalled the end of the prayers and Austin turned to the door. 'You can come in now. They've stopped praying.'

Melissa was happy. It had been very stressful before the

service with Lucy and Wayne not showing up till after the prayers and Lucy was acting very strangely. She kept talking about an accident to anyone who would listen but seemed very unsure about quite what had happened. Wayne, on the other hand, seemed transformed. Melissa had had long arguments with Brian about whether Wayne should be asked to be a godfather to young Gregory.

'I know he's your brother,' Brian had said one night, 'but be honest – he's a wastrel! He spends most of his time down the pub with his mates and you can't rely on him. He'll never take it seriously.' Melissa couldn't find it in herself to disagree, except on this last point.

'I really want him to be asked, Brian. I think he needs responsibility, and I intend to make him aware of what I expect from him when I ask him.' And in the end she had won the argument, because she always did. But she hadn't been sure, especially when Wayne had arrived just minutes before the ceremony. Yet now something seemed different. Back home, with the christening party in full swing, Wayne hadn't touched a beer at all. A glass of orange juice, three-quarters full, sat on the table but he seemed to have eyes only for Gregory, whom he had been holding now for over half an hour. She sat down next to him, suddenly aware of why she was happy.

'I'm glad to see you're getting to know each other,' she said and he looked up at her and smiled, the slight bashful edge to it surprising her.

'I've been thinking,' he said, 'would you mind if I started taking Greg to church sometimes?' Melissa had to stifle a cough as she sipped her white wine.

'Church?' she spluttered, and then smiled. 'Not at all. In fact, I'd be delighted. But . . . why?' Wayne looked kind of sheepish for a moment, as if he was not sure what to say, but then he looked up and into Melissa's eyes.

'It was my fault we were late. I overslept. Actually I had a hangover and Lucy was mad at me and we were running up the church path when a strange bloke stopped us. I think there must be something wrong with him but he guessed who I was and told me . . .' He hesitated, then went on. 'He told me that you think I am a good man and that you're hoping I'll get something out of being godfather to Greg.'

Melissa's eyes widened a little but she said nothing. Wayne looked down at the baby in his arms. 'I'm not a very good man, Mel, but I'd like to be. And being there this morning – something felt right. I think it was the strange bloke to be honest. I reckon that any place that welcomes the likes of him and lets him do what he does would probably welcome me, and it's got to be good for Greg, right? Besides, that bloke's the first person to say something positive about me in weeks. He made me feel good about myself. I owe him something, even if I'm not sure what.'

Melissa couldn't stop herself from smiling this time. 'I tell you what,' she said, planting a huge kiss on his surprised forehead, 'I'll come with you if you like. After all, you're going to need someone to nudge you during those long prayers!'

William Watts was sitting with his brow seriously furrowed, his stewards sitting opposite. 'Of course, I appreciate what Austin does on a Sunday morning,' he said, 'but I'm not at all sure it's appropriate to have him greeting people as they come through the door. We've kind of got used to his ... eccentricities, but heaven only knows what first-timers think encountering him there. I think we should him find a less ... obvious job.' And he looked around the room for agreement.

'Actually, William, I disagree with you there.' Felicity was a quietly spoken woman, but her voice had a certain authority to it when she chose. 'I was talking to that young couple who came yesterday morning – from the christening a couple of weeks ago. It's the mother and her brother I think – he's the godfather to the child. Anyway, I was pleased to see them and asked them what had brought them back since they hadn't come before the christening.' She paused and looked up at Mr Watts. 'It was Austin,' she said. 'He was apparently very nice to the mother, Melissa I think she's called, and the young man, Wayne, he said how welcoming Austin had been and that he was the reason he had come back. In fact he seems to be striking up a friendship with Austin.'

'That's all very well,' Mr Watts said, trying to reassert himself, 'and I'm sure we're all very pleased for Austin, but I'm still not sure we can leave him in that position.'

'William,' said Felicity with as much authority as she could muster. 'I appreciate you have never felt comfortable with Austin. You're far too clever for him and I think his simplicity confuses you. But,' and she emphasized it as if to say 'this is not up for discussion', 'we need people like Austin in responsible roles, where they can be seen to be doing something positive and something useful. And we need them where they can do some good. The church is not just about erudite sermons and a glass of Chablis over a few hands of bridge, you know. It's a living, breathing conglomerate of souls, every one of which has a role to play and a part to fulfil. I'm sorry to disappoint you, William, but on the whole souls are not won through learned preaching but rather by the little acts of kindness and goodness that go quite unnoticed in the normal run of things. But that's what matters to people and that's what defines what type of church we are – not how many different types of worship we can offer but whether we are a friendly, welcoming, caring, and above all, loving community. Austin can claim to have brought two new people into this church. That's two more than I can and I think he deserves to stay in his job, don't you?'

Austin still hated Wednesdays. And Tuesdays and Fridays. But Thursdays had become much more enjoyable since Wayne had started coming round after tea. His mother wasn't sure what to make of Wayne, especially when he suggested that Austin might like to come out to the cinema with him, but she was grateful for the peace and quiet and she didn't object. As for Austin, he was still excited after seeing the latest *Star Wars* last week and couldn't wait to show Wayne his new library book on space ships. He was sure Wayne would like it. Perhaps he would even help him with his new Airfix kit afterwards. Austin thought he probably would. After all, Wayne was a good man.

Reflection

As he looked up, Jesus saw the rich putting their gifts into the temple treasury. He also saw a poor widow put in two very small copper coins. 'I tell you the truth,' he said, 'this poor widow has put in more than all the others.'

Luke 21.1–3

It is so very easy to judge people, even from within a supposedly enlightened body such as a church, but then it can be genuinely hard to value equally the contributions of each and every member. Paul's teaching about the body in 1 Corinthians 12 is well known and is an excellent image of how we should look at ourselves, but if we are honest do any of us really want to be the insignificant parts of the body? After all, we all know that the people at the head – the talented, the eloquent, the popular – are the ones who make a difference ... don't we?

The trouble with that kind of thinking is that it flies in the face of what Jesus taught. Time and again throughout the Gospels we see him turning the accepted values of the day on their head, recognizing the true worth and potential of each and every individual. It may be difficult for us to do the same but it is an essential part of being a Christian. No matter what we think of someone else, God may be working through him or her to change somebody. It may not always be obvious but one small life lived entirely out of the shadow of splendour really can bring the gospel to life.

Lord of the harvest

He sits in the shed, gently stroking the blade across the stone. Around him lie the scattered tools of his trade. It might look chaotic, but he knows where every tool lies, where every pot can be found, where every seed has been stored. He should do. After all, he has worked this shed for many years – boy to youth to man. He knows it intimately. Above his head the rain beats a steady tattoo on the roof, the rhythm counterpointing his movements. Through the window he watches the water falling across the lawn, mentally running through his list of tasks for the day. Whatever the weather chooses to send he will soon be outside, and in his mind's eye he can see himself in the garden, picture each area waiting for his attention. There is so much to be done, so much that needs his care. He shrugs to himself. What will be will be, he thinks, and he returns to the grindstone.

The Green Room is an oasis of calm and tranquillity. Here are drinks and towels, a vase of flowers, today's papers, scattered with casual precision. The room is carefully furnished. A sofa with just the right degree of softness, an easy chair here, there and over there, pastel shades, big cushions. An overhead fan wafts the air lazily downwards, the coolness welcome on his skin. For here he sits, mentally preparing for the show. In his mind he goes over his script, rehearsing the words, refining each movement, until finally he feels ready. He closes his eyes and pictures them in the arena – arms aloft, faces alight, singing and shouting and stamping as the warm-up band does its stuff. He can sense the excitement growing. He can feel the hunger rising. These people need him. These people want him. They need to hear what he has to say. As he sits and prepares for the show the weight of responsibility once again falls upon him and he closes his eyes, seeking inside himself the God whose Word he will bring to this stadium.

She nurses her coffee as if it was life itself. And perhaps it is. The bags beneath her eyes are testament to the hours she keeps, the slight tick a sign of her caffeine addiction. But the coffee is doing its job. She can feel it within her, warming and energizing, and soon she feels stronger, braver, ready for the day. Somewhere in the chaos of her room is her laptop and within it her diary, and having extracted it from beneath a pile of papers she scrolls down the day, silently groaning at each new appointment. Occasionally she wonders, 'Why me?' But the answer is always the same – 'Because . . .' And so she grabs her battered coat, throws the mug, unwashed, to join the others in the sink, and steps out into the hallway. Once again she feels the weight of responsibility upon her shoulders and wonders who she is to be carrying such a burden.

*

The rain has eased off now, falling like a light mist, swirling in the breeze. He stoops over the bed, fork in hand, easing the wet soil up. The weed succumbs to his grasp, reluctantly breaking free from the earth, and he tosses it into his basket. Soon it will join the others on the compost heap. Clearing the space around the flowers his great hands, soil-stained and weather-hardened, are as gentle as a midwife's as he delicately lifts the blooms to check them for blight. Reassured he lets them drop, quietly talking to each one as they fall back into place. He always talks to his blooms – encouragement, praise, sympathy for them in bad weather. As if they were alive, as if they had souls, he pours his care and attention upon them. And week after week, as he gently tends, they grow visibly stronger, healthier. Bud and blossom and bloom. Now he gently pats the fat seedpods. 'Soon,' he whispers, 'soon.' Soon it will be time to collect the seeds. Soon it will be time to gather the harvest. Soon...

He is working hard now, and the sweat is beginning to show on his brow, reflecting the spotlights. He pauses, as he knew he would at this point, and takes a moment to look around the stadium. He has learnt how to read faces, how to judge what lies behind them. He sees those who are ready to be saved, ripe for picking any time now. He sees, too, those who are unsure. They want to be saved, but he needs to work on them further. And then there are those who are lost. Soon they will be irrelevant to him. His work here will be done, and the lost ones will leave. Sad, but inevitable in his world. Only the few will be saved. It is written. And so he concentrates on those few. Crafting his words for maximum effect, he encourages them, praises them, sympathizes with them. As if heaven itself depended on his words he pours himself into their hearts and minds, lifting his voice, milking the emotion, deliberately leading them on and up to his finale. He knows he will win them, as he has so many others over the years. He will carry them over this evening. They will be saved. It's just a matter of time.

Mid-morning, and she holds her coffee mug tightly, inhaling before she drinks. She has sat and listened for three mugs now, occasionally nodding, sometimes speaking herself, but mostly listening. It is, after all, what she does. Day after day she sits and listens to other people's stories – everyday tales of hardship and break-up and struggle. She sits and she listens and she drinks her coffee and day after day she hears the same stories of despair, hears the same themes again and again and again. And day after day she listens and she encourages. Sometimes praising, sometimes sympathizing, she offers care and attention. It's not much, but she sees the difference it makes, for the telling of the tale unlocks people. It frees them to move on, to get over it, to put it behind them. When she comes back the next time the stories are still told but they are less intense, they carry less pain. And week by week she watches them grow stronger, more confident, less troubled. It is what she does.

*

Today the sun shines. From a sky of clearest blue the warmth beats down, almost physical in its intensity. The flowers raise their heads and shake them in the sunshine, their petals streaming like long hair. Their hour has come. They wait for him. He emerges from the shed, bronzed skin naked to the sun, and permits himself a smile. This is the day he has worked for. Through the cold winter months he has nursed. With the coming of spring he has brought them on. And with the coming of summer he has watched them glory. First the buds, then the blooms. Wild and showy, soft and restrained, light and shade. He has painted his garden with the palette of life itself. He has worked with nature, encouraging, bending, shaping. And she has filled his canvas. So today he will make his harvest.

He moves slowly around the garden, looking for the plants with the largest seedpods, the ripest fruit, and gently, ever so gently, he begins to collect. With a tenderness belied by the coarseness of his hands, he prises open the first pod, pouring the black seeds into an envelope. A stroke of the tongue to seal it, a name written on the outside, and he moves on. Each envelope opens to receive a cascade of seeds. Each closes on the promise of new life. From plant to plant he moves, gathering the promise of next year's garden, until at last he is done. Arms full, he makes his way back to the shed, to file the envelopes away. Only then does he sit, glass in hand, and toast the day. As the sun's rays sparkle through the trees, setting his garden aflame, he raises his glass and drinks to the harvest.

*

He is shining like the sun, the spotlights subtly increasing in strength as the moment approaches. The heat they generate beats down on him, almost physical in its intensity. There is no breeze to cool him, but the crowd is moving as if blown by the wind – swaying, whispering, chanting its affirmation. He has them. It is time. And so he begins the harvest. Arms outstretched, he issues the call, invokes the ritual, calls them to him. And they come. Those he has worked so hard to win come forward, a mixture of smiles and tears, confidence and anxiety. And at the front they are gathered by his aides, taken aside to counsellors, promise forms and a new life. He watches the procession, mentally counting the souls, calculating their tithes, and he smiles to himself. It has been a good night, a good harvest. The foundation's bank account will look good tomorrow morning. Later, in the sanctuary of his room, he will drink to that.

She has lost count of how many coffees she has drunk today. This one is fresh-brewed, straight from the filter, with a rich aroma and a lot of caffeine. She drinks deeply, feeling the hot liquid within working through her system, and watches the world go by from her pavement table. The sun is warm – that and the drink making her sweat a little. But she needs the energy, and a little space to sit and just be herself. It was a good meeting. She has sat and listened to the story for weeks now, each time through noting the subtle changes, commenting in slightly different ways. And today all those weeks have borne fruit, all those hours of nodding and empathizing.

Today the story had a different ending. Actually, today the story *had* an ending. Instead of hanging, unresolved, it came to an end. The storyteller finished and moved on. And she could see the difference. She said so. There were tears and laughter and some hugging, and then she left, both of them knowing she would not need to return. And so she sits outside the café, nursing her coffee, watching the world go by. Across the road she reads the sign outside the local church. 'Harvest Festival'. She snorts quietly to herself. In this city? What's the point? What relevance can Harvest have for her? She checks her lap-top to see where she is due next, drains the last of her coffee, and drags herself to her feet.

And all the time He has been watching. He has seen it all, heard it all, and known it even as it has happened.

He has watched the gardener, smiled in remembrance of a story He once told, recognized the love and the dedication that has brought the harvest home. He will listen to grateful thanks for food and provision, for the gifts of nature, and He will accept the praise that is offered. He knows that with nature what will be will be. But He also knows who created nature, who first breathed the breath of life into the world. He knows who made it so and he is content to be Lord of the Harvest.

He has watched the preacher, grimaced in remembrance of a story He once told, recognized the self-gratification and manipulation that has won the harvest of souls. They shine in His eyes, like fresh seeds in the rain. But like the seeds of his story He knows that most will fall fallow, flower briefly, if at all, and fade away. He rejoices for the few who will blossom and bear fruit, but He finds the stadium thanksgiving hard to listen to. So much hope promised, so little that will come to pass.

He has watched her for a long time, and though He has shed tears with her, yet He smiles in remembrance of a story He once told, recognized the love and dedication that has worn her so thin, yet served Him so well. In return she offers Him no thanks, no praise, not even any recognition. But He is content. He remembers creating a garden and placing a man and woman there to work it, knowing that in so doing they would transform it. Today, in the garden of life, He looks for those who are transforming, those who are shaping the world so it bears the mark of their own intelligence, their own art, their own concern. That and the mark of Him whose image they bear. Those who work the land and produce the harvest of festival and song. Those who work to harvest people, to bring them to life, to bring them to fruit. He watches and He smiles, this Lord of the Harvest.

Reflection

Two men went up to the temple to pray, one a Pharisee and the other a tax collector. The Pharisee stood up and prayed about himself: 'God, I thank you that I am not like all other men – robbers, evildoers, adulterers – or even like this tax collector. I fast twice a week and give a tenth of all I get.' But the tax collector stood at

*a distance. He would not even look up to heaven, but
beat his breast and said, 'God, have mercy on me, a
sinner.' I tell you that this man, rather than the other,
went home justified before God.*

Luke 18.10–14

Many of the lessons of Jesus are hard to accept from
within the comfort of a church. It is so easy to think that
because we are Christians we have somehow 'made it' and
that we therefore have a monopoly on God's time and his
affections. But this is not what the Bible teaches. Time and
again Jesus draws our attention to the less obvious places
of the world, the less obvious people, as if to say, 'Look
for me there, too.' The story of the Good Samaritan
reminds us that God is at work outside of the church as
well as within it.

I used to run a fair trading shop, and one of the lines
we had a lot of success with was a range of greetings cards
from a company called Brush Dance. They were
inspirational cards on recycled paper and they sold in
armfuls. The company was founded on strongly ethical
principles and a story explained how it came to choose its
name. The story is a long one but it is sufficient to know
that 'brush dance' comes from a native American Yurok
Indian healing ritual where being true to yourself means
giving your best to help a person in need. Sometimes our
understanding of God can be greatly enhanced by those
who do not know him at all, although as Christians we
have a responsibility not only to be true to ourselves but
also to be true to our calling. Fortunately real abuse of our

faith is a rare thing; however, the story of the Pharisee and
the tax collector is a salutary reminder for us all not to
become too complacent or too arrogant in our religion.
There is always more to learn...

The shawl

It had taken a long time, but at last the pattern was beginning to emerge. Agnes paused a moment and sat back to admire her work, casting a critical eye over the loom but finding nothing to fault. One could never be sure how a pattern would work out when starting on a new piece. Even a pattern that looked good on the page sometimes failed to work when the threads were woven. But this one seemed to be taking on the life and vitality that marked a good design. The colours were working well together, the interlocking lines of the design beginning to show their true complexity, and above all it felt good. Not physically, although the wool was soft and gentle under her fingertips, but somewhere deep inside of her it stirred a primeval satisfaction. Nodding her pleasure to herself she picked up the loom again and continued weaving.

Outside the dull grey morning was lifting, the clouds breaking and burning away, and before long the sun broke through, shining brightly into the room, falling awkwardly on her face. She sighed and raised her voice.

'Susan!' she called, 'Susan!' and waited for a moment until she heard footsteps on the staircase. Settling back into the bed she watched as the door opened and Susan stepped into the room.

'What is it, Agnes?' Brisk, but not unkind.

'It's the sun, dear. It's shining right in my eyes. I always think it's such a shame to shut it out but it's no good, I can't concentrate when it's so bright.'

'No, you're right,' Susan said as she moved to draw the curtains part way across the window. 'It will give you a headache if you let it. There now, how's that?'

'That's lovely, dear. Thank you.'

Susan moved back towards the bed. 'I haven't asked how you are this morning, have I? Has that pain in your back gone?'

'Yes, dear. It's much better now.'

'And what about your legs? Do they still hurt?'

'A little. I try not to move them too much. It hurts when I do.'

Susan nodded, as if that were enough answer, then turned her attention to the loom. 'That's coming on nicely, isn't it? Really pretty colours. What's it going to be?'

Agnes smiled gently. 'It's going to be a shawl. I'm making it for a friend. I wasn't sure about it until this morning, but now I think it's going to come out fine.'

'It's beautiful, Agnes. You have such a gift with that loom. I don't know how you do it.'

'When you're confined to your bed, dear, you find the patience to do all sorts of things.' And the conversation ended there because neither of them could think of a suitable reply.

Back downstairs, Susan allowed her smile to drop

again and went back to the kitchen. She hadn't prepared any food yet and the front room really needed the Hoover running over it, but at least she had managed to put the washing on. Agnes got through so many bedclothes these days that Susan couldn't afford to let it build up. As it was she loathed ironing sheets and had grown to hate the washing basket that invariably greeted her arrival each day. Still, the washing would dry quickly today in the sun. Sighing to herself again, she picked up the potato peeler and started making lunch.

It had been ten months since her life had changed. She had been at church and the vicar had asked the congregation if there was anything special they needed praying for. There was the usual embarrassed silence and then Mary had surprised everyone by saying that she would like prayers for her mother, Agnes. It seemed Agnes was not getting any better, indeed she was steadily getting worse, and Mary didn't think she could leave her now during the day. She had to go to work, though, and so she was going to have to put Agnes into a home. But she knew Agnes would hate that so could they pray for her please? The vicar had incorporated some bland platitude about 'strength to face adversity' into his prayers but Susan had hardly heard it. All she could hear was the sound of her own voice talking to Mary after the service offering to act as a home help for Agnes during the day if it would allow her to stay at home. The look of surprised delight and relief on Mary's face had been enough reward at the time and Susan had gone home feeling as if for once she had done the right thing.

That was ten months ago. Forty weeks. Two hundred

and eighty days. She had started counting. It wasn't as if she didn't like Agnes – for a bedridden old lady she was a delight to be around. Oh, she had her moments, when Susan could quite happily wring her neck but they were few and far between. No, the problem was her, Susan Alice McDonald, and to be honest she wasn't entirely sure what the problem was.

Richard, the vicar, had been very helpful when she had gone to see him. 'I feel useless,' she had said, and had started to tell him how all her life she had felt as if she were not good enough. She wasn't as clever as her sisters, wasn't as good at sports as her friends, wasn't as pretty as the other girls. She'd married Stephen because he'd asked her to and she didn't think she'd get another offer, and he wasn't a bad man and it wasn't really a bad marriage. It just wasn't very exciting. Now the kids had grown up she was on her own again during the day and she felt useless, unfulfilled, wasted even. And most of all she felt lonely.

'I've tried praying about it,' she told the vicar. 'I've lost count of how many times I've prayed for him to take my bad feelings away, for him to bring me a friend, but he hasn't answered my prayers.'

Richard Bates had looked at her for a long moment, his fingers steepled in front of his face in that way of his. Eventually he had lifted his head away from his hands and said, 'Did you always give your children what they asked for?' The question had caught her off guard and she had said 'no' before she had thought about it. 'Exactly,' he had said. 'I doubt if you ignored them, but kids are kids. They don't always ask for the right things.' And he had sat back and smiled as if he had just solved all her problems.

Susan might have been an unexpected answer to Mary's prayer, and for a while she had thought that perhaps helping Agnes was the answer to her own prayers, but now she wasn't so sure. Actually she was sure. She didn't like coming here any more, but she knew she couldn't stop. If she stopped Agnes would have to go into a home and she couldn't be responsible for that. And so she ironed and cooked and washed and cleaned and she assisted Agnes with all the difficult, undignified things that come with being nearly bedridden, and she ought to feel satisfied at the very least. This was true Christian service, wasn't it? Shouldn't she feel that she was finally doing something right?

And yet she didn't. To be honest, she felt guilty. Guilty because she found herself resenting Mary, driving off to work each day and leaving her ageing, difficult mother for Susan to deal with. Guilty because she found herself resenting Agnes, gently demanding care and attention all day. Resentful because she couldn't leave Agnes on her own and so she couldn't go out and meet people and make friends and somehow feel less lonely, and guilty because she realized that she didn't want to be here any more. What was it her own mother used to say? 'You can't change what you are.' That was what she used to say, and it was true. She wasn't good enough to be anything other than a servant, and quite clearly nobody liked her enough to want to be her friend. It was the final irony. She was actually being of use to someone at last, being a companion to them even, making a real contribution. But she still felt useless and she still felt so desperately lonely.

Agnes wasn't sure what she was feeling. These last few weeks had been hard as she had often been in pain but Susan had been so kind and so helpful that it had been bearable. Just. But something looked wrong with Susan and Agnes couldn't quite put her finger on it. She had a leadenness about her movements, as if she were the one in pain, not Agnes. Her smile was always warm, but Agnes could see how brittle it was, how thinly stretched. And once, she was sure, she had heard her crying in the kitchen. She had wanted to ask her about it but when Susan had come back into the room, eyes puffy and red, she had complained about the onions she had been cooking and Agnes hadn't wanted to challenge her. Never mind. The shawl was finally finished. The last fringes had been sewn on this morning and she sat with it on her lap, the colours flowing across the design like molten metal. It was beautiful and Agnes was pleased. It would be just right, she thought. Just right.

Agnes had enjoyed her lunch. Susan was not a great cook but there were some things she did really well and toad-in-the-hole was one of them. It also happened to be one of Agnes' favourites. As Susan bustled into the room to clear away the lunch tray Agnes told her how much she'd enjoyed the meal. The briefest of smiles passed over her face and she nodded her head in acknowledgement, but as she reached to lift the tray from the bed Agnes put a hand on her arm.

'Sit down a minute, dear, would you? I want to talk to

you.' Susan looked a little wary but she put the tray down on the floor and sat on the edge of the bed and waited. After a while Agnes started. 'When I was a little girl my teacher picked me to make a short speech to the whole school at the summer prize-giving. It was only a few words of welcome and it was written down for me, but I was so scared I cried all day before it, and when the time came for the speech I ran away and hid in the toilets! I was never very good with words, you see – even other people's.' Susan just sat and nodded, so Agnes went on. 'I don't think I have ever told you how very, very grateful I am for what you are doing for me. I've said "thank you" often enough, but always for things you've done, never for the – well, for everything. But I am grateful, Susan, more than you can possibly know. And I've got a present for you. A token. Something to remember me by.'

And she reached across the bed and handed Susan the newly finished shawl. 'This is for you, Susan, with my gratitude, and with my love. I never expected to make a new friend at this stage, but I'm so glad you've come into my life. You've been a real answer to prayer.' Agnes stopped. 'Susan, what's wrong?' for Susan was crying. Not just the gentle tears of pleasure at the beauty of the shawl, but real, gulping sobs that shook her body from end to end. 'Susan! Susan, my poor dear...' and she took the sobbing woman in her arms and held her as her tears fell on the bedclothes and the minutes turned into an afternoon.

The dull grey morning was lifting, the clouds breaking and burning away, until the sun finally broke through, bathing the cemetery in warmth and light. Most of the mourners had moved away, heading back to the silent cavalcade of cars, but two figures still stood by the side of the open grave, arms entwined in mutual support. Eventually they turned their backs on the coffin and started walking. 'Thank you, Susan,' said Mary. 'I'm very grateful for your support.' Susan smiled.

'I can't say it was a pleasure,' she said, 'but it was a privilege.' They walked a while in silence and then Susan stopped, her hand on Mary's arm. 'I want to tell you something,' she said. 'Can we sit down for a moment?' She indicated a small bench and the two women moved towards it.

'Your mother was a remarkable woman,' she began, and patted Mary's arm at the sign of the small tear that welled in her eye. 'These last two years have been very draining, but very rewarding. I think if I'd known what I was really offering when I spoke to you after that service I might not have been so keen. But then again . . . ' Susan smiled at the recollection. 'I think I offered to help you for all the wrong reasons. I thought I was doing my Christian duty, something I needed to do back then, but it turned out that it was Agnes who was serving me, not the other way round. All the time I was caring for her physical needs she was ministering to me with a kindness and a patience that I barely noticed until the day she gave me the shawl. Nobody had ever given me anything so beautiful before or anything with so much of themselves in it. And she said it was in thanks for being her friend.

'Do you know, I so desperately wanted a friend and I

hadn't even noticed it had happened? This last year we spent so much time talking. I was afraid you were going to notice the house hadn't been cleaned properly, but you never said anything. We talked about so many things, but we talked a lot about prayer. Agnes always said I was the answer to your prayers but I think in retrospect that she was the answer to mine. She certainly taught me to approach prayer from a different angle. I learnt from her how to begin and end with adoration of God. If she could praise him in the midst of all her suffering then so could I, however difficult life seemed. And I learnt to forgive – other people, yes, but most of all myself. If I'm to love other people even as she loved, then I have to learn to love myself, which meant forgiving myself as well as everyone else. And most of all I learnt not to ask.'

Mary looked quizzical, as Susan paused a moment before going on. 'I don't mean that we should never pray for things, for other people or ourselves,' she said hastily, 'but I used to get so terribly worried about using the right words and I used to find it got in the way of my prayers. Agnes and I were talking about the Lord's Prayer one morning, don't ask me why, and she suddenly said, "Do you realize how simple this prayer really is? There are so many things we could pray for and yet Jesus tells us to ask for just two things for ourselves – bread and forgiveness." I remember that morning so clearly. Her eyes were unusually bright – like sun at the bottom of a well. She looked at me intensely, as if my life depended on her words, and said, "I have learnt throughout my life that God is fully aware of my needs. He knows my hopes. He knows my fears. He knows what ails me and he knows how best to help. I don't need to tell him any of that," she said. "I don't need to put any of it into words. I just need to tell him how much I love him, and how much I depend on him, and he will take care of the rest."'

Susan paused, looking across the neat rows of gravestones. 'As I say, Mary, your mother was a remarkable woman.'

The sun chose that moment to go behind a cloud and a sudden chill swept through the cemetery. Without speaking the two women stood, Mary straightening her coat as she started walking back to the cars. Susan stood for a moment by the bench, looking back one last time to the open grave. Finally she smiled a sad smile of farewell and pulled the brightly coloured shawl closer around her shoulders. 'God bless you, Agnes,' she whispered, and left her friend to the earth.

Reflection

So do not worry, saying, 'What shall we eat?' or 'What shall we drink?' or 'What shall we wear?' For the pagans run after all these things, and your heavenly Father knows that you need them. But seek first his kingdom and his righteousness, and all these things will be given to you as well. Therefore do not worry about tomorrow, for tomorrow will worry about itself. Each day has enough trouble of its own.

Matthew 6.31–4

Learning to pray is in many ways a skill to be acquired like any other. But the assumption that the beautifully crafted sentences and phrases we hear from the pulpit most Sundays is the only valid model is to deny ourselves much of what prayer is about. Like a friendship or a relationship where words are not always necessary to convey our feelings, so too words are not always necessary with God. If ever we fear we do not know how to talk to him we need only read Jesus' words in the Sermon on the Mount to reassure ourselves that he is way ahead of us.

But prayer is not always about leaving things with God, unburdening ourselves of our problems. Sometimes prayer is about accepting that we have a responsibility to help bring about something for which we are praying. The Church has always struggled with the concept of 'ministry' but it has come to a far richer understanding in the past few years than it used to have, truly beginning to embrace the notion of the 'priesthood of all believers'. Without in any way minimizing the roles that our ordained ministers fulfil we have come to recognize that all of us have a ministerial role to play, indeed that the kingdom of God will only come about when we all accept our call to ministry in the widest sense. And yet there is still more to learn, not least that so often ministry is a two-way process, of benefit both to the one being ministered to and the one doing the ministering. It can be blessed to give, for sure, but we must never lose sight of the fact that it can be equally blessed to receive.

Grace

The underpass is dark – dark and wet. The concrete columns rise around him like some sort of cathedral, vaulting heavenwards with a determined confidence, dwarfing him in the process. He clutches the damp edge of his sleeping bag and wraps it around his body, seeking a warmth that is not there. Beside him his dog stretches and whimpers quietly and he reaches down to stroke its neck with a world-weary affection. Somehow the sense of touch calms its hunger and it pushes into him, moulding into his contours with accustomed familiarity. He accepts the animal warmth with a mute gratitude, unconsciously shaping himself to accommodate the creature. Closing his eyes he seeks a few hours' escape in sleep but it is not to be. Tired his body may be but it will not succumb to sleep this night and so he lies by his dog, listening to the traffic on the flyover, seeking within its roar a lullaby that is not there.

As the hours pass the roar subsides into an occasional growl and his dog sleeps fitfully. But for him there is no release. He watches as the pubs close and people spill out onto the pavements, laughing and talking as they wend their way home. Later he watches as the clubs gently eject their late-night clientele, unsteady footsteps a measure of the good time. The smell of the late-night burger bar taunts him as he huddles closer to his dog. Onions, hot dogs, beefburgers, chips. He tries to think of something else, but the smell is so...insistent. Despite the rain, despite the cold, it wraps itself around him more effectively than his bag. It is no comfort, only a quiet kind of torture. In an earlier life he would have despised such junk food but tonight he craves it with the fierce longing of one who knows it is beyond his reach. Silently he gathers what remains of his will and forces the craving aside.

She comes from somewhere in the cathedral but he does not see where. Like a gossamer vision she floats down the nave, her dress flowing around her legs like a sea mist. Long blonde hair hangs around her face and her lips, full and sensuous, frame a perfect smile. An angel, he thinks. And then a start at the thought that it might be his time. His dog kicks, woken by his movements, in turn bringing him to reality, and he sees it is no angel, but simply a woman that walks towards him. An attractive woman, certainly. Beautiful if truth be told, but not breathtakingly so. More the plain, ordinary beauty of one whose body is simply *right*. One who is comfortable in her self, happy with who and what she is. As she draws near he withdraws into himself, trying to make himself small, trying to remove himself from the presence of such beauty. Yet she sees him still, making for him unerringly, her smile drawing wider as she nears. Finally he has no option but to look up, to acknowledge her presence, and his eyes travel appreciatively up her legs towards the pleasures of her body. And there he finds she is holding something, holding it out towards him, her smile inviting him to take it. Beefburger! And chips! Hesitantly he reaches up, ashamed at his need, suddenly aware of his smell, his eyes finally meeting hers, and in the meeting all hesitation is gone. This is for you, those eyes say, with no strings, no conditions and he gratefully accepts it, tearing at the paper as his dog stirs and whines hungrily. There is enough for two and soon they are sharing the meal, oblivious to the angel as she continues her gossamer walk up the aisle and into the night.

They named her Grace, after her great-great-grandmother. There was no thought as to what the name might mean. It was just a pretty sound, an old-fashioned name and weren't such names in vogue? They never thought of the theological meaning, of the terrible burden such a child would have in living up to such a naming. Yet Grace became the epitome of her name. As a child she was good-natured, well behaved, possessing manners that set her apart. But as an adult she was everything the name could have hoped for. Where her looks came from was unclear. As she grew older her father became more and more convinced she couldn't be his. But then he would look at his wife and realize that such a girl shouldn't spring from her loins either. She moved with the practised ease of a model, gliding elegantly across the floor, sashaying without trying. Her mannerisms were delicate and, well, graceful. She was even of temperament, gentle and placid, yet surprisingly resilient. All in all, a credit to her parents. It's just a shame they weren't a credit to her.

Mick and Sandra had been friends from junior school days, so when they eventually married everyone remarked how sweet it was. Unfortunately by the time Sandra was pregnant and they had to tie the knot they were already bored with each other. Everlasting love was great while they hardly knew each other but the magic of living together, of sharing everything, soon palled and they fell into a bitchy state of mutual antagonism. Perhaps there was a kernel of something good at the heart of their relationship, for they never separated, but it was no atmosphere in which to bring up a child. Grace learnt her swearwords young, learnt how words can hurt, how they can wound and damage, how they can cauterize. She learnt how to manipulate, how to anger, how to irritate. She learnt how to stifle encouragement, how to belittle achievement, how to denigrate success. She learnt it all, but she never used it. Great-great-grandmother must have watched over her, for in truth she grew in grace and beauty, all the wiser for her upbringing but showing none of its marks. Unlike her parents she achieved well at school. Unlike her parents she went on to further education. Unlike her parents she did not believe in true love. Perhaps that is why she found it.

He was a student of theology. Tall and thin with those little round spectacles that made him look a little like an inquisitive rodent. His background could not have been more different. Roland was the sixth child of Dennis and Marjorie. With his father in the forces he had grown used to moving every few years and had lived in Hong Kong and Singapore as well as half a dozen locations in Britain.

Unlike his father and the rest of his brothers he was not blessed with the muscles of Hercules. Nor did he have their chiselled good looks, their sun-kissed olive skin, healthy complexion and perfect teeth. He was his mother's boy and maybe this accounted for his quiet, almost introspective nature. It certainly explained why he did not follow his brothers into Sandhurst but chose instead an obscure theological college in Oxford. There, away from the shadow of his family, he blossomed in his own quiet way. Always interested in Christianity, he joined the Christian Union and became deeply involved in his first year, but as his studies drove him deeper into the realms of belief he found the student gathering too restrictive, too conservative. Over the first summer break he found a job in a local bookstore and explored the local church scene a little, eventually settling into a medium-sized Baptist church with a liberal female minister. She recognized a questioning soul and made sure Roland was invited to lunch with those of her congregation who loved to debate theology.

In the second year his tutors noted a substantial improvement in his grades. When they questioned him he confessed to the benefit of being able to work out some of the more tortuous theological issues with people who were actually trying to live with them in the real world. Raising eyebrows at the implied criticism they nevertheless acknowledged that something had improved his thinking and increased his marks accordingly.

Strangely, Grace never went to church. But she did buy a lot of books, or at least she spent a lot of time in bookshops, which is almost the same thing. And while flicking through the latest Terry Pratchett she would glance up at the young man behind the counter who was so obviously staring at her until he blushed and dropped his pen. As she reached the counter to make a purchase he was nervous and a little sweaty, looking even more like a rodent than usual, and when she asked him if he was busy that evening he dropped his pen all over again and had to grovel under the counter to pick it up.

None of her friends could understand why she went with Roland. Even his name sounded a little ridiculous to them and not one of them could see what she saw in him, but then most of them were dating rugby players called Gareth or members of the rowing club, and their ideas of beauty were less flexible than those of Grace. It was one of the reasons he loved her. Quite apart from the sheer surprise at having such an attractive woman love him, fancy him even, he soon came to understand that for Grace there was no 'classic' definition of beauty. She saw it even in the ugliest things, the most unlikely situations.

Take her family, for instance. He met her parents on a weekend visit to her home and instantly disliked them, but then so did most people. They were rude, crude and decidedly unwelcoming. They clearly disapproved of their daughter's choice of boyfriend and for that matter did not seem all that approving of her, referring several times to her 'poncy' college and 'student ways'. He could not understand why she would want to spend time with them but she simply answered that they were her parents and she loved them. Besides, she told him, they weren't as bad as they seemed. He thought that no one could be that bad but he didn't share his thought. He just marvelled once again at Grace's ability to see beauty in anything.

Like Maurice, for example. Roland had been friends with Maurice since the first weekend of college. They had hit it off from the first time they bumped into each other and had looked for accommodation together at the end of the first year. Student accommodation being what it was they ended up in a squalid flat designed for a small single person, somewhere on the edge of town.

It was then that Maurice began to change. Roland was never sure who was responsible for starting the rot but Maurice went out one night, ostensibly on his own, and did not come back. In itself that was not entirely unusual so Roland thought nothing of it, but when the day passed without any sign of him and then another night he began to get worried. Eventually on the second day he was just about to call the police when Maurice walked in. Actually 'swaggered' would be a better word. Roland could see immediately there was something changed about Maurice but it was only over the following days that he came to understand the reason, and the reason was drugs.

Some people take drugs all their lives and never seem to experience any change other than a gentle high. Others take one dose and are forever different. Maurice was one such. Roland found him suddenly prone to mood swings. His temper seemed to have no fuse at all. He drifted through the days in a kind of casual haze that left no time for cleaning up after himself, no time for bathing, no time for friendship. Within a matter of weeks Roland came to heartily loathe his former friend. Fortunately for him it was about this time that Grace arrived in his life and he could at least escape, having found a soulmate upon which to pour out his anger (and his hurt). And he left nothing out. Soon Grace was as intimately acquainted with Maurice's unpleasant habits as was Roland, but whereas he had simply washed his hands of his former friend, she was not like that.

She started trying to talk to Maurice whenever she was at the flat, but Roland became so annoyed about it that she started calling round when she knew Roland was out. At first Maurice thought his luck was in but she quickly forestalled that impression and thereafter they actually became quite good friends. But it was not an easy friendship. In truth Maurice had become a self-centred, opinionated, drug-addled and rather unpleasant person. There was very little about him any more that might draw someone to him and if pushed to name his friends at that time he would eventually have had to admit that Grace was the only one.

Roland, of course, was incandescent when he found out and it nearly cost him his relationship with Grace, but in the end he realized it was impossible to be angry with her for any length of time. Instead he talked to her, tried to find out what on earth she was playing at going behind his back to spend time with that . . . that *thing* that shared his flat. But when she talked to him it was as though there was a symphony orchestra playing in the background –

everything sounded reasonable and sensible and smooth and soft and his anger just melted away. He realized that it was simply her nature to make an effort with people like Maurice and once he was satisfied that it didn't threaten their relationship he left her to it.

And she changed him. It took several months of talking to him, of sitting with him, of holding him sometimes. It took numerous walks in the park, a number of very late-night telephone calls and once she even slapped him when he went too far. But gradually she got through to him. She took the ugly thing that he had become and she restored it, if not to beauty, then at least to that rugged state of acceptable manliness that passed as a decent human being. And she managed to do it without damaging her relationship with Roland. Indeed, as he begrudgingly began to admit that Maurice wasn't quite as obnoxious as he had been, his admiration for and love of Grace grew ever deeper. He even began to rebuild the friendship with Maurice and in later years would happily tell anyone who was prepared to listen how Grace had brought them back together again. Maurice rarely talked to anyone about that time, but he knew how much he owed her and always made sure he remembered to send her flowers each year on her birthday.

And all this time Roland went to his church and Grace didn't and he came to accept that that was the way she was and he didn't push it. He found himself getting more involved as his faith became stronger, joining a housegroup among other activities, but Grace never begrudged him the time he spent with his 'church' friends.

It was the housegroup he most liked, though, that excited him the most. Once every couple of weeks he would meet with eight or so other church people and they would tussle away at some point of theology or some burning issue of the day. He enjoyed the cut and thrust of the arguments, the mental stimulation of it all, but in truth he also learnt much about his faith through this group and he often used it to try and clarify his understanding.

One week they got talking about salvation. Roland was quite certain he had been saved from a life he would not have been happy in by coming to study at the college, but was not so sure how to understand salvation in the wider sense. When one of the other members trotted out the mantra that all were saved by faith through the grace of God, Veronica startled everyone a little by saying that that was all very well but what was 'grace' anyway? She pointed out that they merrily used the words of the Grace every time they met but what did it really mean to talk about the 'grace of God', or to wish it one upon another?

One of the older members of the housegroup said that Grace was simply the undeserved love of God. There was no need for God to act as he does towards men and women, indeed from all the evidence of history we should deserve anger or judgement rather than love and kindness, but it was the nature of God to give freely. And nowhere, someone else pointed out, was this more clearly demonstrated than in the coming of Jesus. The human race did not deserve salvation yet Christ died regardless, God's free gift of unconditional love. That was grace. The group sat for a while, aware that although they had rehearsed the theology correctly something was still missing, a feeling finally expressed by Veronica when she said that understanding the theology was one thing, but at a practical level what could grace mean to her? How could she make it part of her daily living? It was then in an instant that Roland suddenly understood, as his theology and his life fell into perfect harmony.

Unconditional love is all very well, Roland told them, but it's very hard for a human heart, so dedicated to conditional love, to understand. But God was not hindered by human feelings of selfishness and jealousy and envy and anger. Nor did he carry around prejudice and bigotry and judgement by assumption. Instead God looked at each person and saw not what they were but what they could be. He saw not the ugliness but the potential for beauty. And more than that, God was in the habit of taking that ugliness and turning it into beauty. And how did Roland know this, his housegroup friends asked, surprised at his sudden intensity? He just smiled and told them about his Grace, about the fact that she was the epitome of her name, showing by the way she lived how the grace of God could be a living reality in this world. And they listened and they nodded and they understood.

In the underpass cathedral he watches as she walks her gossamer walk back into the shadows, leaving her offering of hot food in his hands. Gratefully he takes huge bites, offering part to his salivating dog. It is warmer tonight and the windows of the local pub are open, the music drifting out across the street, the words of the song washing over him as he eats, ignored as he savours the hot juices.

> Grace –
> It's her name
> It's her way.
> My Grace...

Reflection

And God raised us up with Christ and seated us with him in the heavenly realms in Christ Jesus, in order that in the coming ages he might show the incomparable riches of his grace, expressed in his kindness to us in Christ Jesus. For it is by grace you have been saved, through faith – and this not from yourselves, it is the gift of God – not by works, so that no-one can boast. For we are God's workmanship, created in Christ Jesus to do good works, which God prepared in advance for us to do.

Ephesians 2.6–10

My favourite story in all the Gospels is found in John 8 – the story of the woman caught in adultery. Not everyone would agree, but for me this has always represented the very essence of Jesus' ministry. Here was a woman who had clearly done something wrong and yet Jesus does not condemn her. He looks beyond the sin, beyond what she so clearly is right now, and instead he sees her potential – what she could become. As a result he offers her forgiveness, and a gentle warning to mend her ways and he sets her on her way. I suspect she was never quite the same again, but then I guess that most of us who have felt the touch of grace feel the same way. Knowing that God accepts us just as we are, without any preconditions, is tremendously liberating. There is no question of our having to change before he will love us and welcome us into his arms. He takes us warts and all and only then starts to make us into something truly beautiful. It gives us all hope.

Theology is never easy. On the one hand we need it to try and encapsulate our faith – to define the parameters, and give it shape and meaning. Yet on the other hand very few of us can think in theological terms. Our faith is instinctive, responsive – something we feel rather than quantify – and so theology can seem distant and abstract and hard to grasp. But we should remember that virtually all theology has practical implications for the way we live our lives. If God looks upon us with the eyes of love and offers us his grace without precondition then, if we are to live as we have been taught, we must seek to offer that same grace to those whom we encounter. We will quickly discover just how hard that can be: we are only human and prey to all the prejudices and emotional judgements that come with our humanity. But if the kingdom of God is ever to come about we will all need to take the ugly things of this world and work with them until they have been transformed into something beautiful.

Coming to life

She had thought the hard part was over, but this was proving far more difficult than she imagined. Not that she had thought about it much. You don't think about burying your son, not even while he's dying. You just get on with the business of watching him die. It went on for ever. If he was in pain then she must have shared every part of it. God in heaven, she didn't know anything could hurt that much! To stand by, helpless, while he fought the pain, while he struggled to die with dignity, while he failed on both counts – a mother should not have to endure that. He was her flesh and blood, and though they might have drifted apart a little her heart was still full of love for him. Aching love. A love that seared itself into her soul. A love that consumes her, even now. It's why she struggles on, even though all she wants to do is stop and cry – cry until she has no more tears left inside, until the pain has passed on, cry for the rest of her life.

Finally it is done. His body lies upon the stone ledge, the shroud caressing it lightly. She must leave him now for the Sabbath is almost here, but he will still be lying there on Sunday to anoint and embalm. Her friends roll the stone across the entrance and it is as if a knife cuts into her, finally taking him away. She staggers and a hand grasps her arm. Time to go home. Time to let the tears come. Time to give in to the pain.

She sits alone in the room, the television flickering unwatched in the corner. Her eyes have been fixed on the same spot for an hour now, maybe longer. There's nothing to see, but then she isn't looking. All her sight is turned inwards, to the past, to her memories. The tickets for their safari lie in her lap, the ink slightly smudged where her tears have fallen. It was to have been their silver wedding and he had surprised her one evening with an envelope and a bottle of champagne. 'Something to look forward to,' he had said, and had grinned when she opened it and found the vouchers inside. She had cried then, but they were tears of excitement and joy, not the sort she shed when the police came to call.

An accident, they said. He wouldn't have felt any pain. He wouldn't have known about it. But it came to the same thing. She was alone and the love of her life had been taken away from her. Their hopes and dreams and expectations had been smashed along with his windscreen and her heart was as broken as his body. She had been today to identify it and she had expected it to be hard, but not as hard as that. To see the body lying on the slab, and realizing that he wasn't there to hear her 'goodbye', nearly broke her. It was just a shell – the vessel that had once been filled with his life and soul and energy. But he had moved on and she would have to find peace another way. The tears come again, but they are not healing her.

*

Even now her mind is racing. She sits, breathing deeply of the morning air, trying to make sense of what she has seen and heard, trying to find a place for it in her heart. All through the Sabbath she has observed the rite of mourning, ridden the pain, accepting it, even welcoming it as part of the healing process. Her friends have been with her, talking her through the events of the last week, forcing more tears to her swollen eyes. And she embraced them, knowing that they acted with kindness, cauterizing her heart. So much pain, but so much love around her that she found a kind of strength, a still, calm centre upon which to stand.

It was how she came here this morning. She should have waited for her friends. She knew that. How was she going to move the stone without their strength? And yet she came alone, at dawn, so she could have him to herself for a little while. Strange that the other women had all felt the same, had all done the same. Yet none of them were prepared to find the tomb empty. At first it seemed they were mistaken, that they had the wrong tomb, but their bottles were still there from Friday, inside the cave. Even the shroud was there, lying upon the slab. But there was no body. No trace, no indication. She had thought the pain was under control up till then but to know his body had been taken cut through her like nothing else. It was all she had left! A shell, for sure, but the shell that had held her son. And it was gone!

And then, in the middle of her pain, came a warmth and a light and a strange comfort, and it was him! A mother knows her son. It couldn't be, and yet it was! The leaping of her heart told her that. Even though she didn't embrace him (strange that, it should have been her first impulse), or even touch him, she was still certain it was him – alive! Alive! So what now for her broken heart? The pain cannot be taken away – it is part of her now – but what has taken its place? Dare she accept this joy? And so she sits. The others have run off to tell the men. Soon there will be people all round, but she needs time to think. She needs to understand. She needs to believe.

The crematorium has such a lovely view. She thought that when she first attended a cremation and she thought it again today as they entered the tiny chapel. It was full – standing room only – but ask her who was present and she cannot tell you. She saw only the coffin, knowing that the shell lay within. She knew without any doubt that he wasn't there any more and yet she couldn't take her eyes off it. And when the vicar said the final words and had pressed the button and the curtains had swung round, taking him finally away from her, she had broken down. Uncontrollable. Inconsolable. They had almost carried her out.

Now she feels foolish, that she made a spectacle of herself. No one said as much, but she knows what she would have thought in their place. And yet they don't understand. It wasn't the loss of the body that set her off. It wasn't the traditional 'last moment' grief, for that is the whole point. She hasn't had a last moment. The curtain and the coffin were merely the final confirmation that she would not be able to say goodbye to him. Somehow he had slipped away from her, leaving no chance of a proper farewell. And somehow, that matters.

*

It doesn't make sense. That he is alive there can be no doubt. So many people have seen him now that it's hard to argue against them. Not that she would, for she saw him, too. Just the once, though, and that doesn't make sense. Why appear just once to your mother? Hasn't she earned the right to see him more than that? His friends, those who have followed him these last three years – they are full of stories of their 'risen Lord'; on the beach, in the room, on the mountain. But to his mother... just the once, in the garden. Why? And then there are the other stories that don't make sense. He might have come to his friends in the upper room – Thomas even got to feel the wounds to compound his belief – but they seem to forget that the room was locked. He appeared without any announcement and no one can say how he got there. What kind of man walks through walls?

But it seems to be his way since leaving the tomb. Lots of people have seen him, but he comes and goes and no one sees where. It just doesn't make sense. If he is alive, why can't he stay overnight? Why does he appear within a room? How does he do that? Yet if he isn't alive, how can he eat and drink? How can they touch him? How can he leave footprints in the sand? The joy she feels at knowing he is alive once more is inevitably tempered by the confusion. This resurrection is not easy. It raises as many questions as it answers, leaves her as confused as she was before his death. It just doesn't make sense.

Her friends have noticed. They have commented how well she looks, how well she is recovering. They mean she looks happy, but they still can't bring themselves to use the word in her presence. 'Too soon,' they whisper among themselves. It's as if the shadow of death must preclude all happiness while it persists. But she has learnt differently, and no one is more surprised than she.

At first she was inconsolable, but not for the reasons they all thought. She could live without him. It was hard. It was very hard. Every day hurt. But she could do it. No, it was the lack of farewell that hung over her, the sense that he had gone and she had not blessed his passing. That was what she couldn't get over. That was what had hung before her like a great wall.

Ask her now when it changed and she is not certain, but changed it has. Maybe it was while she was sorting through his drawers, folding clothes, sorting socks. There was a familiarity there that was comforting. Or maybe it was as she flicked through the photo albums one evening. Memories of holidays and family gatherings rose from the prints, laughter echoing around her. For a moment she thought she heard him speak her name, but it was surely only memory. Later she spoke with friends about him. They all had memories they treasured and they were anxious to share them. Things he had said, things he had done. She found herself laughing and she caught herself speaking about him in the present tense.

But it was her son who finally did it – him and his blessed music. Always too loud, though lately she fancied it had mellowed a little. She had been sitting, going through her jewellery box, remembering when he had bought each piece for her, when she became aware of the lyrics of a song coming through the wall. 'No one truly leaves you if you live in their heart and mind.' Her mind dismissed it as trite, but her heart leapt in understanding, and she chose to listen to her heart. Much to her surprise it made perfect sense! She was living in his heart and mind. Still. Even now. To tell the truth, they had been so much a part of one another, she realized, that she could never extract herself, never be apart from him, even if he no longer shared her bed or held her hand as they walked. It made perfect sense. And it made all the difference.

So yes, she is happy now and if they won't use the word, well she will. Not 'over it'. Not yet, not while it's still raw and she has to get used to doing things on her own. But she understands now that she didn't miss the chance to say 'goodbye' to him. She didn't miss saying 'goodbye' because he never really left her. And that is enough. She can live with that.

He is gone. She is certain of it now. And yet she finds she is happy. His friends came to see her this evening, the story overflowing even as they entered her home. Gradually she managed to calm them enough to piece together the tale. The mountain and the cloud, the voice and an ascension. And so he is gone, taken away from her a second time. Only this time it doesn't hurt so much. It even makes a kind of sense to her, if not to his friends just yet, for she has had time to think. While they were meeting him and eating with him and fishing with him she was sitting and trying to make sense of it all. And it was working. She was his mother after all. Of all the people in the world who knew him, she knew him best. She knew how he thought, how he felt, what he believed, and she has come to understand him.

The others will come to it too, in time. For now they are too excited by what they have seen, but she has seen to the very heart of it. He came to her once, in the garden, because he wanted her to know he lived. But he did not come to her again for he knew this new life was not like his old. In truth he did not belong here any more. The world was too small a place to contain him. She had just lost her son and to have him back only to lose him again . . . It was better that she know, but that he keep his distance. So typical of him, she thought and smiled, always thinking of the wider picture. And her hurt at his distance was as nothing compared to what she would have felt at a second loss.

So it is that she can see why he did what he did, and she can see what he has become. The signs were there all along if you looked; a physical presence that could interact with the world around him, real interaction from a real person, a force that could – that *will*, she is certain – affect the earth and everyone in it. But also a spiritual presence – a body that comes and goes of its own will, that is not held by this earth, that is not bound by it.

They told her what he had said to them on the mountainside. 'I will be with you.' And so he will. She is certain of it. She can see how it will be. Physical. Real. Powerful. Present. A constant source of comfort and strength. And yet one with his father, as close to them as their prayers, at once within them and around them. More than flesh, more than Spirit. Ascended. Finally she understands what Resurrection is about. Finally she understands that everything in his life, every part of it, has been leading to this point. Finally she knows that he never came to her again because he never really left her and never will. And that is more than enough. She can live with that. After all, countless millions of others will.

Reflection

In their fright the women bowed down with their faces to the ground, but the men said to them, 'Why do you look for the living among the dead? He is not here; he has risen! Remember how he told you, while he was still with you in Galilee: "the Son of Man must be delivered into the hands of sinful men, be crucified and on the third day be raised again"'. Then they remembered his words.

Luke 24.5–8

There is a common assumption in the Church that Easter is a happy time, a time of light triumphing over darkness, to be celebrated in smiles and laughter and flowers and song. And there is a lot of truth in that. All these elements should be part of our celebration. But to see only the light misses the whole point, for Easter was not an easy experience for anyone caught up in the events. We are used to death. We may never find it easy or ordinary but we see enough of it in our lives and encounter it often enough at least to understand it, even if the pain of it still tears at us. But how does one come to terms with Resurrection? How do we come to terms with a dead man alive once more and yet alive in a way that we do not fully recognize? It must have been so hard for those who were closest to Jesus, and for me, although it remains the fundamental core of my faith, the foundation of all I believe, the Resurrection challenges me with as many questions as it answers.

As Christians we all look forward to the resurrection of our souls into eternal life, but there are many other ways in which resurrection can have meaning for us in the here and now. The resurrection of a life from despondency and despair into acceptance and peace is just one such example. But we can all draw strength from the message Easter teaches us: even in the depths of darkness there is a light. Indeed to me the very darkness of Easter is what makes the light ultimately shine all the brighter and gives it its real splendour. It is one of the great truths of our faith that however dark our lives may seem to be, God is always there, patiently waiting to bring us once more to life.

Made again

It was the light that was so strange. She couldn't put her finger on why but it didn't seem right. It didn't seem to come from anywhere and perhaps that was it. No source. Soft, diffuse, like silk lying over everything. Venice had been like this, only everything there had looked old and faded. The plaster had fallen from the walls and had not been replaced. On every building there was evidence of the corrosive powers of the water that dominated the city. It was all run-down and scruffy and rather disappointing in close-up. But bathed in the soft, almost other-worldly light it all took on a gentle majesty that was beautiful to behold. It captivated the senses, ravished the eyes and worked its way indelibly into the memory. This was like Venice, except it was all so much cleaner, fresher, as if someone had taken the whole place apart and rebuilt it exactly as it had been but had used brand new materials. It had that 'scrubbed' look, fresh-washed and sparkling in the soft light. She felt new here, as if the whole world had been created afresh, just for her. As if *she* had been created anew. And she knew that it was just a dream, that soon she would wake up as she had done so many times before. Wake up, to the pain and the frustration and the depression.

The sounds of the village woke her. As she opened her eyes and the aches in her body exerted themselves once again she lay still, listening to the noises all around her. Children were playing somewhere close, their early-morning game full of shrieks and laughter. Mburu was already walking his ox to its day's work. She could hear its complaining grunts as he herded it down the road. Even now, this early, the insects were abroad, their constant background whine something you just got used to. Groaning quietly to herself she reluctantly dragged her body upright and mentally set her face to the new day.

'I'm so glad you're going,' her vicar had said when she'd told him of her appointment to Uganda. 'You'll have a wonderful time and do wonderful things!'

'It's only for a year,' she'd replied, 'and I'll only be working in one location.'

'I know that,' he had told her, 'but I still believe you will make a difference. It's what God wants you to do, and you should never underestimate God.' She had often thought of those words these last few months. 'What God wants...' She tried to remember that whenever she felt that she wasn't getting anywhere, which was most of the time, tried to remember how confident she felt that it *was* God's will for her to be here. But if she was honest she really wasn't sure any more.

At first it had been easy. Mburu had been there at the airport and she had liked him immediately, his whiter-than-white smile flashing across the concourse like a beacon to her loneliness. He had welcomed her, spoken of his hopes for what she would do, what she would be able to achieve for his people, and had led her gently to the taxi and then to the hotel. That was the last time she had slept well and it was over eight months ago. Now she had got used to the heat and the noises in her hut, used to the insects and creatures that scuttled all night, used to the uncomfortable bed, and she slept in fits. Never all the way through the night, but in and out of sleep, in and out of her dream, in and out of her bright, new world.

In her aches and pains her body still carried signs of the illness that had struck her so fiercely after the first few weeks. She had nearly died then, she knew now. They hadn't told her at the time but Becky (she could never pronounce her real name properly) had since said they had been very worried.

'We held a prayer meeting for you,' she had said one afternoon while they were walking back from a visit to the next village. 'We thought you was dying and we didn't know what else to do. So we prayed together – nearly the whole village was there – prayed that you would get better.' She had flashed her familiar smile again. 'And you did! We knew God could not let you die. He has too many plans for you.'

Plans. Yes, she remembers she had plans when she came out here. She was going to make a difference. She was single-handedly going to change the lives of all these people, transform the village and everyone in it. Hell, why not be honest? She was going to transform the whole damn area! Well, she had soon learnt otherwise, even before her illness had reminded her abruptly of her own fragility. It seemed so arrogant now, so conceited to think she could ever have made a difference. She was too small. She knew that now. She was just one person, inadequately trained, under-resourced, and with a whole village full of people looking to her as if she were the Second Coming. She shook her head, trying to shake out the depression. Yesterday. Now yesterday had been a bit better...

She had walked six miles to a village on the edge of her responsibility (she always walked – it was that or not go at all), and Miriam had been waiting for her. How Miriam knew she was coming she had no idea. She had only decided to go that morning, but she had promised to call back and check on Elieru. It was several months since she had last been and the memory still haunted her. Miriam had lost her husband last year. She was no weakling, that was for sure, but the loss of Yunib had hit her hard and left her nearly destitute. With a young boy to support and his newborn sister to look after Miriam had had no time to work – no opportunity – and the family had rapidly spiralled into poverty. The memory of their tiny home, their generosity as they insisted she share their frugal lunch, had embossed itself into her mind and she had left promising that she would try to help them, even though she didn't really know how. This time Miriam had embraced her like an old friend as soon as she was close enough, smiling all the time.

'I want to show you a thing,' she had said, picking up young Mysutu. Without waiting for a response she had led her across the village to where her tiny shack stood, surrounded by a small field. 'Look!' Miriam had said, pointing, and she had followed the finger to find herself looking up and into the eyes of a cow. 'Elieru has named her "Ida", after you,' she said. 'I hope you won't be offended.'

Ida shook her head. 'Is this the one?' she asked.

'Of course it's the one!' Miriam had almost laughed back. 'Those people from Send A Cow – they listen to your plea. They hear what you say about me and they send me a cow! Now I milk her every day and I sell the milk. I sell it! I have money to send Elieru to school and I have enough left to pay for my field to be ploughed and to buy seed. She's a good cow. She even gives me dung for the ground!' And Ida had laughed, genuine laughter for the pleasure of seeing this woman's life transformed by the simple addition of a cow. She hadn't expected this. She had written a couple of letters, made a call to the relevant people in London and they had made the usual non-committal noises. 'Well, we are very stretched at the moment . . .' and she'd known that nothing would come of it. And yet here it was. A tiny victory among everything else.

As she left her shelter this morning she met Nathaniel and walked with him to the village well. She was going to talk but the seconds turned into minutes and nothing came to mind so they walked in silence, her depression quietly leaking out of her body.

'You are quiet,' he observed after some five minutes had passed without either of them speaking. And it was as if he had opened a sluice gate. Without stopping to think everything had poured out of her and she had told him how she felt. How her body ached constantly with the after-effects of her illness. How she knew she was achieving nothing. How she couldn't live up to the expectations that had been put upon her. How she would never be able to face going back and explaining that she had done so little after such high hopes had been raised. She had talked and talked and talked and Nathaniel had listened, at first as they walked, and then as they stood by the well and finally as they sat beneath the great tree in the centre of the village. When she had finished he sat in silence some more and then looked at her and started speaking.

'I had a dream once,' he said, 'many years ago. In my dream I saw the village. I walked through its huts. I walked by the people, though they did not see me. And I was saddened by what I saw for what I saw was the truth – I saw the village as it was. But then in my dream I saw the village change and before my eyes it was made again. The dwelling places were rebuilt and they shone in the sunlight. A well was dug and they were able to draw clean water. The fields were ploughed and planted and started to bear crops – full, healthy crops that were harvested. The animals were plump and well fed and the people – ah, the people were smiling! They were smiling because they were happy. They had food to eat, they were healthy. They even had the money to send their children to school and to buy new seed. And in my dream I cried out, "Who will make this so?" And do you know who answered me?' She shook her head. 'God himself answered me. "I will make it so," he said. That was my dream.'

Nathaniel stopped to look around him. 'It seems to

me,' he said after a while, 'that God has chosen to make our village anew through many people. And the strange thing is, they have all felt inadequate, that they have somehow failed because they did not transform our village themselves. And yet we are transformed. Each of you has played your part and you cannot know how you have changed us, for much of the benefit is felt after you are gone. But without you, without your friends at home who support you in their own, small ways, none of this would be any different.' He sat for a while, absorbing her silence, and then turned to ask her, 'Do you believe the book of Revelation?'

The question surprised her. 'I don't know,' she said after a while. 'It's a rather confusing book. I guess I don't...'

'A pity,' he said. 'There is a lot of truth in it. "I am making everything new." That's what God says. That's what he is doing here. With a little help from people like you.'

She walked through the city of her dreams once again, but this time without waking. For the first time since she arrived she slept through the night. Funny, she thought, it doesn't *look* like Jerusalem. Truth to tell, it still looked a bit like Venice, only cleaner and fresher, still bathed in the soft, silk light, still exquisite. Only there *was* a difference, she realized. There were people here, all around, and they were people she knew! There was Miriam, with Elieru and Mysutu, her eyes sparkling with pride as she stroked Ida, her cow! There was Mburu, his smile reflecting the light like a marble pavement. There was Becky, her quiet, gentle concern radiating from her like a beacon on a misty coast. And here was Nathaniel, standing, arms outstretched, as if he could wrap them around the city and clasp it to his chest. And she suddenly realized why she felt comfortable here, why it felt so good simply to walk among the buildings, mingle with the people. It felt good, because she had helped to build it!

In her dream she walked contentedly into the bright new morning that beckoned her, knowing that she had been made again. No – knowing that the *whole world* had been made again. And though it was just a dream, she smiled as she slept because she knew it would come to be.

Reflection

Then I saw a new heaven and a new earth, for the first heaven and the first earth had passed away...I saw the Holy City, the new Jerusalem, coming down out of heaven from God, prepared as a bride beautifully dressed for her husband. And I heard a loud voice from the throne saying, 'Now the dwelling of God is with men, and he will live with them. They will be his people and God himself will be with them and be their God. He will wipe every tear from their eyes. There will be no more death or mourning or crying or pain, for the old order of things has passed away...I am making everything new!'

Revelation 21.1–5

'What difference can I make?' is a question we often hear. As individuals in society we wonder how our voice can be heard, whether our individual vote can make the slightest difference to the outcome of an election. As individuals in the world we respond to news of another famine or disaster with the resigned shrug of one who knows the issue is so huge, so vast, that our few pounds can never be noticed. And as Christians it is so easy to look at the world and wonder whether there is any point praying for anything. One tiny voice in the wilderness. Would God even notice if we did not pray? Yet the strongest chain begins with a single link. Each one may be insignificant in itself but if any one link breaks the whole chain is compromised.

We believe that God has a vision for our world, that it is his will that it should be a place of equality and justice, of opportunity and fulfilment. In the book of Revelation the prophet looks forward to such a time and a place and a beautiful place it is too. But Jesus told us that the Kingdom was 'at hand', that it was something we could build here and now upon this earth, and he was a great believer in the greatness of the small. It should not matter that we do not see the result of our work. What matters is that we do what is right, what we believe God has called us to do, and ensure that our part of the chain remains strong. Chances are that someone, somewhere, will notice the difference.

The Giving

Unlock your imagination...

It was one of those summers. Glorious and sunny by day, hot and humid by night and, try as I would, I could not get to sleep. The pillow had become an enveloping, suffocating thing and the sheets were restrictive and claustrophobic. With the windows open, nightcaps duly taken, boring books fiercely read, still I could not sleep. So I lay there in the dark gradually becoming more and more alert even as my body screamed out for rest. Eventually the frustration became too much and I decided the only thing to do was go out for a walk to see if fresh air and exercise would bring sleep. Trying not to look at the clock I slipped into some clothes and crept out of the house, not really sure where I would go, just letting instinct guide the way. In the early morning stillness everything seemed strange – peaceful and other-worldly – and I met no one else to disturb my enjoyment of the night and the darkness.

Bath is a city built in a deep valley, and without consciously choosing I soon found myself high on one of its hills, looking down over the buildings below. Streetlights twinkled in the stillness and the silence seemed to amplify what few sounds there were. As I stood still I could hear the water tumbling over Pultney Weir, more than half a mile away. The sound was calming and reassuring, a gentle and persistent backdrop to the occasional bark of a fox. Time ceased to exist and I stood, entranced by the stillness and the beauty of it all.

It is difficult to say when I first became aware of the noise. Faint at first, like a canvas slowly flapping in a gentle breeze, but gradually growing louder and more regular as I looked upwards to find its source. There, high above me, was a pure white bird, soaring gracefully around and down, its wings flapping slowly in the night sky. It seemed impossibly graceful and I stood staring up at it as it grew larger and larger – until, with a growing sense of unease, I realized it had too many legs. It was then I knew I must have been dreaming for it suddenly dawned on me that what I was watching was no bird, but a horse – a pure white horse with wings – a Pegasus, straight from the mists of legend, alive and circling above me, spiralling down. Completely captivated by its effortless grace and beauty I stood transfixed as it touched the ground, stepping down as if it had merely reached the bottom of a staircase. But then it walked over to where I stood and I swear it bowed to me before it spoke in a voice as rich and as deep as a living legend should be.

'Hail, son of Adam,' it said. 'Well met in this magical hour.'

And since on hearing the voice any doubts I may have had simply evaporated I returned the greeting and then, 'Is this real?'

'As real as the rest of your life,' said the Pegasus.

'Except that you . . . you don't exist!' I couldn't help but say it, the Pegasus smiling at my discomfort.

'Yet here I am, and here you are. Can you deny the evidence of your own eyes?'

'No,' I said dubiously, 'but I could be dreaming and you could be a figment of my imagination.'

'Just because I lie beyond your usual daily experience?'

'It does seem the most likely explanation.'

The Pegasus looked thoughtful for a moment.

'Would you ascribe any event or happening that was outside your usual experience to an active imagination?' it asked, and I had to agree that probably I would. 'I see,' said the Pegasus. 'So the northern lights would be a figment of your imagination, would they?'

'Well . . .'

'As would being mugged, presumably.'

'Pardon?'

'And spiritual healing?'

'No!' I said. 'That is . . . I mean . . .' But I was lost and the Pegasus knew it.

'Your lives are much deeper than you imagine,' it said, like a teacher gently imparting great wisdom. 'You live only in the shallow end of your three-dimensional human existence and yet you cannot package everything you encounter into neat, clearly defined boxes of pre-experience. You need to accept the realm of Mystery. You must acknowledge the potential for the unexplained and unexplainable. You must leave space in your lives for the supernatural, for you must live not just in the physical world, but also in the spiritual. If you do not, if you wrap yourself in your humanity, how can you ever soar beyond yourself and encounter He Who Made You?'

'That makes a kind of sense,' I said somewhat reluctantly, and the Pegasus smiled its encouragement.

'Trust in your experience,' it said. 'Let go and see the world through the Maker's eyes. You'll see a lot more.'

For a while we were silent, but curiosity got the better of me eventually. 'What are you doing here?'

'Resting,' said the Pegasus, 'and gaining my bearings. I'm on my way to a party and I needed to check the way.'

'Whose party?'

'Ah. It's a surprise birthday party, I suppose. Would you like to come?' The question caught me off guard and I began to make excuses – after all, it was late and I was supposed to be asleep – but the Pegasus assured me it wasn't far and promised to see me home safely. Eventually I smiled. 'Oh, why not. You lead the way.'

'No,' said the Pegasus. 'When I said it wasn't far I meant it wasn't far for me. We'll have to fly. You get to ride, I do the work.' Before I could protest it knelt down before me, saying, 'Climb onto my back,' and then, as if it could read my thoughts, 'You won't fall. Trust me.' Settling into the impossibly soft, almost down-like skin, I fought back my fears, part of my mind laughing hysterically at what I was doing. But as my heart pounded, the Pegasus spread its wings, huge snow white feathers unfurling gracefully, majestically to either side of me, and with a slight spring and the gentlest of flapping we soared into the night sky.

The city quickly receded below us, the lights twinkling

like animal eyes in the dark. Then, with an unexpected 'crack' of its wings the landscape suddenly blurred and we soared through the deep midnight blue of a star-filled sky. Below us occasional glimpses of land only served to confuse me further – great cliffs and seas, snow-capped mountains, vast plains, all fading in and out of clear vision.

'What's happening?' I shouted.

'Don't worry,' came the answer. 'I travel through space *and* time. It will ease in a few minutes.' I hung on tighter, closing my eyes and trying desperately hard to accept the realm of Mystery, until suddenly there was another 'crack' from the wings. When I opened my eyes the blur had vanished, to be replaced by bright moonlight, a tropical ocean and, beneath us as we circled, an island. It had wide, sandy beaches, palm trees along the shore, and there was a fire burning on one of them with figures moving around it.

'It's beautiful,' I said.

'I knew you'd like it,' replied the Pegasus, and with a sudden banking movement we dropped quickly but gently, landing on the beach a few hundred yards from the fire. 'Now,' said the Pegasus, 'shall we join the fun?'

Together we walked across the sand towards the bonfire, and as we approached it became obvious there was indeed a party going on. I could see figures dancing in the firelight. I could hear voices raised in song and conversation. I could hear music – rhythmic, pulsing and wild, yet soft and gentle at the same time. But as we drew near I realized with a strange lack of surprise that the figures dancing were not all human. Even as I walked with a Pegasus I saw humans, yes, but also other creatures of legend – Satyrs, Fauns, Centaurs and, best of all, a great, silvery Unicorn – all frolicking in the moonlight, capering around the fire with a pure abandon born of joy and anticipation. Before long I could resist no longer and I joined the dance, following where instinct led – sometimes wild and frenetic, sometimes slow and reflective. All the time laughing or singing or reflecting the unspeakable pleasure of being alive, celebrating the very gift of life in the oldest of languages. In this way we danced for who knows how long. Hours? Days? And yet the moon did not set and the fire never dimmed, and the stars still shone and the tide never went out.

Eventually we sat to one side, drinking coconut milk, relaxing in the cool night air.

'You were right,' I said. 'I do like it. It's beautiful.'

'That's good,' said the Pegasus. 'I like to know those I bring here see the same beauty that I do. It is said beauty is in the eye of the beholder, but true beauty is always beautiful.'

'You said this was a birthday party. Whose birthday is it?' but the Pegasus just smiled.

'You'll soon see. It's nearly time, just be patient a little longer.' We waited in silence for a while, the beach now quiet as all the revellers sat and waited.

'What brings you here?' I asked. The Pegasus looked at me, its eyes as deep as mountain lakes.

'I hear the Maker calling me, calling me to the Giving, the giving of himself. The call is strong, so very strong. It echoes around the hills. It echoes back and forth through

74

time. It resonates in the valleys and in the oceans, calling alike to city and to village, industrial wasteland and moorland. And I cannot refuse the call. It is the Maker's voice that calls me, calls me by name to the Giving.'

The Pegasus paused. 'What is this Giving?' I asked. 'What's being given?'

In response the Pegasus climbed to its feet. 'Our power is limited,' it said, 'and in that respect we are very like you. We are individuals. We are free to live our lives in the manner of our choosing. We are free to control our own destiny. But we choose to walk in the Maker's footsteps. We choose to let our destiny be entwined with his. And we cannot do that in our own strength.'

'What do you mean?'

'Hush! The time is here. You'll see.'

Somehow the atmosphere thickened tangibly and the creatures around the fire stood up, anticipation clearly in their faces – peaceful, smiling, beautiful. Then, as I watched, the fire took on a different hue. Suddenly it burned silver, bright and clean with no smoke and, I realized later, no heat. A single note, rich in resonance and pure and strong came from somewhere undefined, and before my eyes the fire changed shape. Now it burned brightly, but instead of squat and low it burned tall and thin, gently stretching upwards and then outwards until I could have sworn it resembled a cross. The music grew louder, unearthly yet not in the least bit frightening, more reassuring, comforting, as if to say, Peace. Be still. Rest. Relax. Open up. Let go. And I did.

As I watched, the fire divided, smaller flames gently

detaching themselves and floating in the air, moving towards each creature and human. I looked at the Pegasus, his face shining, and not just with reflected flame. Then I realized that there was a flame for me too. My heart leapt in anticipation as the flame hung above my head. Suddenly the note changed from restful to triumphant and as one all the flames dropped. Without fear I waited until the flame kissed my forehead and then it was as if a surge of power shot through me. Flames flickered about me, with no heat, no pain, but within my blood flowed strong, my muscles flexed, my senses exploded, every sight and sound and smell and taste and texture magnified strongly and my heart burned within – a warm sort of heat – a kind of a glow.

As suddenly as it came, it went, and we were still on the beach, the fire burning as before, the moon shining, the sea lapping. Only now there was gathering noise as the people and the creatures started laughing and shouting and dancing and running.

'Come on!' shouted the Pegasus, 'Follow me!' and it took off at a gallop down the beach.

'Hey!' I yelled, 'I can't keep up with that!' But to my surprise I broke into a run, quickly catching it up. 'I'll race you,' I laughed, and with a slight yelp of pleasure it took up the challenge. Neck and neck we raced along the beach, mile after mile, the cool night air drifting against our faces, never tiring. Laughing together we ran for the joy of running, once more celebrating life itself, running and running till eventually we collapsed on the beach and let the warm waves wash our feet.

'What was that?' I panted, and the Pegasus looked at me.

'Have you never encountered the power of Pentecost?'

'Pentecost? But that's a Christian festival and you...'

'Yes?'

'Nothing,' I said.

'You thought that we would have nothing to do with a Christian festival?'

'I suppose so. I always thought you were part of something that wasn't really Christian at all. You know. Magic. Fairy-tale. Legend. That sort of stuff.'

'That is often where we are found,' said the Pegasus, 'but the truth is we belong to that place which is neither here nor there, neither now nor then, neither real nor unreal. We belong to the realm of Imagination. And perhaps we see things as they really are. We know the earth has a strength, a presence. Call it Mother Nature if you like, but you could equally well call it a soul. We know too that there are powers in the world that you have lost the art of knowing. For all your modern achievements you are still largely blind to the spiritual world. You want everything explained in scientific terms. You want laws and equations to govern everything, to make it safe and controllable, to make it comfortable. You do not want to know about the wild side, about the Maker's side. You have forgotten, or choose not to know. But we know that Power and Soul are the Maker's gifts. The complexities of the universe exist because the Maker wills them so to do and because He sustains them.

'And in the Giving that sustenance reaches perfection. The Maker gives himself, his very presence, offered to his creation. His power to run in our veins. His warmth to burn in our hearts. His strength to hold us steady. His light to guide our way. His love to enfold and protect us. The gift is given, the ultimate gift of the Maker himself. You say Pentecost is just a Christian festival, but I wonder how many of you realize its true power and its importance, not just to those of you who celebrate it, but to the very fabric of the universe. It is the Maker's doorway into the world.'

We sat and looked at the stars, twinkling in the deep blue night sky, listening to the sea, happy to be silent. Soon the Pegasus stirred.

'Time to go,' it said, and not without a certain reluctance I climbed once more onto its back, no fear this time, exhilaration coursing through me as its wings spread and we soared majestically into the night sky. Below I saw the light of the fire still burning, flickers of movement around it suggesting the others were still dancing.

'Don't they know when to stop?' I asked.

'The party never stops,' said the Pegasus. 'It is always Pentecost.'

'What do you mean? We celebrate it just once a year.' The Pegasus smiled.

'Once you have encountered the Pentecost, once you have known the Power, you see its source in all things and you learn to draw its strength wherever you are. I am not of your world. I must return to the Giving to restore my strength. But you, son of Adam, are closer to the Maker. You reflect his image and as such the Power is yours as you need it. For you, every day can be Pentecost. Once the discovery is made and the channel is opened you need never be short of its strength.'

'But you never told me whose birthday it was,' I yelled.

'Haven't you realized yet?' cried the Pegasus. 'It was yours!' And with a 'crack' of wings the landscape blurred, tiredness finally overcame me and I drifted into sleep.

Late in the morning I awoke feeling refreshed and alive. I was in my own bed, at home, everything as it should be. Slightly sorrowfully I thought of the Pegasus and of the island and of the Giving. Is this real? I had asked. Obviously not. Just a dream. But what a dream! Swinging myself out of bed something caught my foot, soft and sharp at the same time. Looking down I saw a flash of white and bent to pick up a pure, beautifully formed feather, noticing as I did so that the carpet was covered with a fine layer of...yes, sand! Suddenly I felt like laughing, or crying, or singing or maybe dancing, but then I somehow knew why I felt so good.

It was my heart. It felt...it felt strangely warmed.

Reflection

Suddenly a sound like the blowing of a violent wind came from heaven and filled the whole house where they were sitting. They saw what seemed to be tongues of fire that separated and came to rest on each of them. All of them were filled with the Holy Spirit...

Acts 2.2–4

The Church has always struggled with Pentecost. With every other festival there is a human element, even if there is a miraculous colouring to events, but with Pentecost we have moved unequivocally into the realm of the supernatural and there is no escaping it. The Holy Spirit is at once the most mysterious and possibly the most wonderful part of the Trinity but it cannot be dealt with coldly and rationally. It is fire. It is wildness. It is power. And it can be scary until we understand it. Our modern way of thinking does not really allow us to consider the supernatural and yet coming to terms with the spiritual world and the possibility of the miraculous is fundamental to being a Christian.

It is also important not to get too caught up in the seasonality of our faith. We celebrate Pentecost just once a year but to limit its power to a weekend in June is a serious mistake. The account of the first Pentecost in Acts sets the pattern for us, but we need to accept that the Holy Spirit is given to us whenever and wherever we need it. For us every day can be Pentecost, if we can only open our imagination and see the world as it really is.

Were you there?

Watch. Look closely now. The TV news is replaying the grand entrance to Jerusalem from earlier today. The camera-shot is widescreen, taken from the helicopter circling above the procession. Down below the streets and squares look like a huge, abstract carpet pattern, but as the camera begins to pan in the jumble resolves itself into individual buildings and gardens. And there! A figure at the centre of the crowd on some sort of animal, moving slowly through the human sea, barely visible beneath a canopy of waving branches. Quite a sight. Extra-ordinary. Of course, you saw all this at lunchtime, watching half-heartedly over the rim of your teacup, but one image from that broadcast compels you to watch again, every frame this time of vital interest.

Now the camera is close, within the crowd, jostling heads and bodies obscuring the view, conveying the sense of excitement, of carnival. Soon the view cuts to a rooftop position, looking down over the heads of the crowd, his face still sometimes obscured by palm-leaves as they wave by. But the camera finds a way through, looking from directly in front, focusing on just his face. It is weather-lined and friendly, a perpetual smile softening the features.

It is a face that speaks in itself, and you find echoes of his best-known sayings running through your mind. You've heard them many times before, read them in headlines, remarked upon them in pubs. It doesn't take long these days for things to enter folklore. The camera seems close. You can almost hear his calm, measured breathing, and when he looks up, straight into the lens, you feel as though the look was meant for you and you alone.

Now comes the analysis: What does the carpenter mean to today's society? What impact has he had in the provinces? Why come now, to Jerusalem? What will be the political impact? How do the religious authorities feel about it? Why is the crowd there and who do they think he is? And so they begin the interviews.

Here is a woman who claims he healed her son. Here a man who claims he was present when he fed five thousand people with a single packed lunch. This man speaks for many in the crowd when he talks enthusiastically about the folk-teacher Jesus, and as the interviews proceed you are not surprised to hear someone use the term 'Messiah'. Most surprising of all is the interview with the priest. Not exactly threatening, after all that would be inappropriate for a holy man. No, more measured, perhaps. But there, behind the words, in that look – you can see violence in those eyes, and you can't help feeling that this is all going to end in tears.

Now the reporter is back in the crowd, trying to get close, trying to put these questions of intent to the man himself. It's not easy, but she's good at her job and she insinuates herself through the crowd until she's close, part of the procession, just behind the donkey. She's calling his name now, trying to attract his attention. Perhaps he doesn't hear in all the noise, though you somehow feel that there's nothing he doesn't hear. But still, he doesn't respond, so she tries the direct approach, hurling her questions at him from behind, challenging him, offering him the chance to put his point of view.

But interested as you would be in his answers, this is where you stop listening to the words, for coming up is the image you remember – in the background, part of the crowd, just beyond Jesus, shouting and waving with the rest... There! There it is. Just a few short seconds on the screen but you are ready for it, watching, looking. The face in the crowd, the face that commands your attention, is your own. And now you see it for the second time you are more certain. It could be your twin, so alike it is. It even moves in the same way, waves like you would wave, looks where you would look. Except – except you know it can't be you. This is Jerusalem on what the media are already calling 'Palm Sunday', and you know. You were never there.

The papers are full of it this morning. All over the front page, special features inside, pages two to seven covered with photos and analysis and interviews and comment. It seems he's really made an impact this time, but whether for good or ill you're not sure. Not yet.

Of course, everyone knows what kind of a place the Temple is. You go because you have to go. It is where God is worshipped. Always has been. Yet it's never really felt very holy, or special, or sacred. The inner sanctum, well, yes – there's always been that sense of Presence there, but since access to it is so restricted it's bound to feel different. But the rest of it? Shouldn't the Temple feel sacred, even in its outer halls? Shouldn't you be aware of the presence of God as you walk through the main doorway – the sense of tradition, of the worshipping people of God, somehow imbuing the very walls, the very structure with the stamp of the sacred? Shouldn't such presence radiate out from the building into the streets and the squares around it, announcing to the world, 'Here is God! Come and worship him'? And yet all you feel most weeks is cheap. As you fight your way past the traders, decline the offers of the salesmen, ignore the call of the moneylenders, it doesn't feel sacred. And when you have to engage them, to buy a sacrifice or change some money, you really resent being cheated, being taken advantage of like that. But you can't complain. No one does. They are Temple. Inviolable. Beyond your reach. Except in your mind, and there you've done all sorts.

So the photos of Jesus tearing through the Temple stalls like a mad dervish bring a quiet thrill of satisfaction to you. Quite a disturbance he caused – a lot of damage. Stalls overturned, goods scattered and smashed, money sent flying into the crowd, and surprisingly little of it recovered. 'Thieves!' he had called them, a word you have thought of many times but never dared to utter. And here! See the photo of him driving them out, with a whip of all things. In one decisive act he has caught the mood of the city, voiced what most have thought but kept to themselves, done what you have wanted to do but never could. The headline says it all in direct quotation: 'This is My Father's House, But You Have Made it a Den of Thieves!' He has made many friends by doing this, but it is certain he has made enemies of the Temple authorities. Dangerous enemies he may live to regret.

You turn to page four, scanning the columns for more information, but it is the picture halfway down that grabs your attention. There! A particularly graphic image of Jesus, whip in hand, herding the stallholders and moneylenders like so many sheep or goats. The men look frightened, terrified even, but the look in his eyes is not vicious or aggressive. Angry, yes, but the hard, clean anger of one who has the Right. But it's not him or them that holds you, stunned. It is the figure in the background. It's you again, clear as day, managing to look vaguely horrified at what the priests will call desecration, but actually radiating exaltation, if you know how to interpret the look in your eyes. And that is what's so convincing about it. You know it's you in the picture. Except – except you also know that you were at home that day. You know exactly where you were and it wasn't there. You know it can't have been you.

You were never there.

Logic tells you not to be so stupid. Logically there must be a rational explanation. It stands to reason. You know where you have been. You know where you were at any given time, and you know that, whatever it looked like, you have never been that close to Jesus. Whoever it was it wasn't you. You were never there. But still...It didn't matter so much in those scenes of the crowd as he arrived in Jerusalem, riding that donkey. There was a happy, festival feel to the whole event. You would have liked to have been there. The same in the Temple – despite the violence there was a feel-good atmosphere to the whole episode. You wouldn't have minded being there, even though you know you weren't. This, though – this is different. Disturbing. Uncomfortable.

First there was that video footage of the trial. Well, they called it that even though you, with no legal knowledge, could see he never stood a chance. You should have guessed as soon as the video relay was announced. Quite unprecedented. Such courts are always held behind closed doors. But this blaze of publicity is as shocking as secrecy. It's almost indecent, such exposure, almost as if the priests were desperate to convince you they were acting by the book. Anxious. Frightened. Above blame.

You sat, enthralled by the spectacle, and found yourself strangely moved by his quiet dignity. Not exactly resignation, more like acceptance. So you were pleased when things didn't go the way the priests planned. As you watched events unfold throughout the night, moving first to the palace, then back to the court, then on to Pilate's residence, you became caught up in them, a sense of importance growing inside you. And you wanted him to get off, to be acquitted. You thought he had when Pilate finally turned his fate over to the crowd. You had seen them around the donkey. You knew how popular he was. And you knew they would save him. So when they shouted, 'Crucify him!' the words hit you with almost physical force. 'Crucify him!' You felt winded. 'Crucify him!' You felt sick. 'Crucify him! Crucify him! Crucify him!' A litany of hate and my, how the camera loves a mob. How it loves to linger on each face, framed with vitriol, lined with (surprisingly), fear, demanding death.

But there! That's what makes you really sick. That image – that one, callous person with violence in their eyes, howling crucifixion at his passive acceptance. That person is you. And this time you know it. There is a sense that tells you beyond doubt it is you. This time you are sure. You were never there, and yet... it is you. What follows is even worse, more disturbing still.

Later in the day the cameras are at Calvary, and though they tactfully look elsewhere while the nails are being driven through the flesh and the blood is spurting and the crosses are lowered into their sockets with a hollow boom, soon they return to dwell on the tortured features of the hanging men. Medical analysis every half-hour, interviews with the onlookers, that sort of thing. The other two with him are making a lot of noise. That is normal. The pain of crucifixion is so intense most can't help channelling the agony into sounds – violent cries, pitiful yelps, begging, pleading, then cursing. Of course, the authorities are not without compassion, and after a couple of hours they offer the drug: sweet numbness, partial oblivion on a sponge. Take it and drift away to die in a quieter place where you cannot hear the abuse of the crowd, the mockery and the laughter, where the pain becomes just a dull, quiet ache, filling the hours to death.

They accept it, pathetically drinking, their final coherent action. But he refuses. All this time he has made no sound, made no response. You know he is in pain. His face, his kindly, weather-lined face, is distorted in a grimace of agony that speaks of pain so deep it goes beyond mere physical hurt. And the camera wants you to experience every flinch, every involuntary contraction, every tortured expression. You know how they like to present their coverage these days: they want you to feel involved, to make you feel like you're one of the crowd, like you're really there.

So it doesn't come as a surprise, this time, when you spot yourself, near the foot of his cross, clear as day. You were almost expecting it. And again, you cannot deny it. Logic might tell you that it can't be you, that you were never there, and you cannot argue with logic. Yet there is a part of you, somewhere deep within, which you are only now discovering, that says, 'Yes! I recognize this place. I have been here. I belong here.' The worst of it is that you are part of the crowd who is mocking him, reminding him of his claim to be able to destroy the Temple and rebuild it in three days; laughing at his claims to be able to save others, when so obviously powerless to save himself. Somehow you recognize this place, and you are ashamed of the admission.

You wish, oh how much you wish, you could say you were never there, even though it would be true.

So you are confused? That is understandable, I suppose, but it needs addressing. You see, there's an important issue at stake here, something central to faith. Your faith. Our faith. At core is the question, how could you have been there? You know what happened is history. Whatever you read or watch, however it is presented, you know it belongs two thousand years in the past. These are events of record, of biblical narrative, of truth and faith. They have no place in the here, in the now, in today's news, and you have no place within them. You were not there. You were not even born. You can accept no responsibility for the shape of what happened. No responsibility at all. And yet here is the untruth. You may not have been there, you may indeed have the excuse of history, of intervening millennia, but nevertheless you are not free of responsibility.

Why do you think of these events as history? The truth is that the pages of a book do not bind the passion narrative. It happens. It occurs. It is now. Tradition and scripture establish the pattern, but to place it in time, at a specific point in time, in past time, is a serious error. Such consignment to ages past denies its power, constrains its truth, limits its potential. And this is a truth that has no constraints, that exceeds limitation, that cannot be denied.

You see, a God who created time does not become bound by it. It's hard for us, caught in the perpetual passing of the moment, to grasp the true nature of God, but for him time is not a cage. When he plans, he plans for all time. When he moves, his movements echo throughout time. And when he gives himself to die upon a cross, it is not only those who saw him die who must take responsibility. Those few hundred people were not enough reason for the Son of God to die. We cannot blame them, comfortable as it would be to do so. Our part in the passion narrative is every bit as real as those who witnessed it. Only the rejection of God by all people, across all time, could lead to his death, and we reject him daily. Oh, not in our words, maybe, but by our actions, by our thoughts, by our lives.

So understand this. As Jesus Christ, the Son of God, dies again in silent agony on a cross, understand that it is your face he sees through the pain, your voice he hears, your life he gains. For you are part of the story. In fact, in a very real sense, this passion narrative is your story.

And while you can say in all honesty you were never there, and there could be no denying such an obvious statement of fact, the truth of the matter is that you *are* there, in this moment, and in tomorrow's. You are there. And this is a truth that will always be.

Reflection

Jesus called out with a loud voice, 'Father, into your hands I commit my spirit.' When he had said this, he breathed his last. The centurion, seeing what had happened, praised God and said, 'surely this was a righteous man.' When all the people who had gathered to witness this sight saw what took place, they beat their breasts and went away.

Luke 23.47–48

It is perhaps the biggest problem in Christianity. No matter how we try to square the circle we always come back to the fact that the actual events that are so crucial to our faith happened two thousand years ago. How can they have any relevance to our lives today? How can they be anything other than merely a fascinating history lesson? There have been dramas, books and films that have attempted to show us what it would have been like to live through those days but no matter how realistic they are we are still left with the comforting escape clause – I wasn't there, so I can't be held responsible. I wouldn't have shouted 'Crucify him!'

But that is thinking that is conditioned by linear time and by the constraints of being human. We need to remind ourselves that God is beyond any of those limitations. We do not need to have been in the crucifixion crowd to be partly responsible for what happened to Jesus. But equally we do not need to have been there in the garden for the reality of resurrection to make a difference in our lives.

It may be two thousand years since Christ was crucified but we are still right to ask the question, were you there? Just be honest with the answer.

The potter's wheel

Chuckles the clown stood by the cowering parents, having herded them into a corner of the room. They smiled, tightly, as he lifted the bucket and turned to the children behind him.

'Well, boys and girls,' he asked, 'what shall I do with this bucket of water? Shall I throw it over them?' The adults flinched noticeably but the children squealed in pleasure and anticipation. 'Yes! Yes! Can I do it? Please? Yes!'

'You're very naughty children,' Chuckles said, not very convincingly, 'but if you say so...' and he drew the bucket back. 'Altogether now! One, Two...'

A lone mother broke the cowering silence. 'No! You'll ruin my hair!' But she was too late.

'Three!' As one, the adults cringed, but all that came out of the bucket was a spray of glitter and confetti that hung in the air for a moment and then fluttered down upon their flinching backs and heads. As one, the children roared with laughter, and Chuckles led them round the room in a silly, skipping dance and a suitably meaningless song. In the corner the grown-ups gathered as much of their dignity as they could muster and muttered to themselves.

'This had better be worth it,' one of them said to his neighbour. 'I took a half-day off work to be here.'

'Well, if it's any consolation the kids are having a whale of a time,' said another. 'Megan will be talking about this party for weeks. By the way, you've got glitter in your hair.'

Half an hour of banal songs, awful jokes and several custard pies later Chuckles waved his final farewells to the room of applauding children, took one last face-dive over his extra-long shoes and clambered into his camper van, laughter still ringing in his ears. He closed the door, slumped onto the bench and pulled off his large red nose.

'God, I hate children!' he stated. And then, as if to make sure, 'Did you hear me, God? I said I hate children.' There was no answer, however, so he sat himself down in front of his mirror and started the process of removing the make-up. With weary strokes of his hands he gradually removed the big, smiley mouth and sparkling eyes, scrubbing down the base layers, until the face that stared back at him was that of a pale, thin-lipped man in his forties, eyes deep and hollow and mouth slightly turned down. He sat and looked at himself for a few minutes and then sighed. 'Either you never listen to me,' he said quietly, under his breath, 'or you must have a really warped sense of humour.' Shaking his head he tidied his things away and changed out of his clown costume before stepping out of the camper van to look for the hostess and settle his bill. The party was just winding up as he re-entered the hall, the children saying their goodbyes and leaving with their parents. None of them gave him a second glance. He was just another dull grey adult. He found Katrina, the mother of the birthday boy, and hovered until she was free.

'Mr Rufus,' she said as she came up to him, 'thank you so much. You were wonderful and the kids adored you. You have a real talent with them, you know.'

Tom Rufus smiled professionally back at her.

'Thank you,' he said. 'That's very kind, but I'm quite tired now, so if we could just settle the account...'

'Of course,' she said, reaching for her handbag. 'I've written you a cheque if that's all right, but, um, here's a little extra for being so good with them all.' She leaned forward a little, a conspiratorial look in her eyes. 'I think Janine and Ralph are going to have to come up with something pretty special to top this when their Daniel turns eight.' She smiled with a fierce satisfaction and Tom responded with a practised smile of his own.

'Yes, well. Glad to be of service,' he muttered, and turned to leave.

'Oh! Mr Chuckles? I'm sorry, that's not your name I know, but I don't know your real name and... well, um... have you got a minute, please?' He looked up to see one of the mothers, hovering just beyond reach.

'I'm in a bit of a hurry,' he started to say, but she gushed on, nervously running her hand through her long hair.

'I understand. Need to get away. But this will only take a moment. I promise.' She paused and looked so expectant, so like the children he had entertained earlier, that he relented, mentally hating himself for doing so.

'Well, if you're quick then.' He moved closer to her, walking with her towards the exit. She was a slim, nervy woman, he observed, constantly fidgeting, her hand often reaching for her hair.

'I was watching today,' she said. 'You were good.'

'Thanks,' he said, rather too shortly.

'No, I mean really good,' she insisted. She paused a moment, stopping in her tracks, forcing him to stop and turn towards her. 'My son,' and she hesitated as if the idea of her son was painful, 'he's handicapped. Down's syndrome. You probably noticed.' He nodded. He had spotted there was a Down's kid among them, it was true, but he hadn't made any special concession. He was paid to do his act, not nurse kids who shouldn't be there. 'Paul is not always...easy,' the woman was saying. 'I know Down's children are supposed to be lovely, and he is basically good-natured, but I really find him...hard work.' She swallowed as if she shouldn't be saying such a thing. 'I really struggle with him,' she said. 'I never know what to do with him, but this afternoon' – and she looked up at Tom – 'you were marvellous with him. He loved everything you did. It was so physical, so direct, it spoke to him in a way that I don't seem to be able to.' She looked down for a moment, as if composing herself. 'He has had such a good time this afternoon and I have you to thank for it. It will make my life easier for a few days and you can't begin to imagine how grateful I am. I just – I just wanted you to know.'

It shouldn't have been a long drive home. He rarely needed to travel more than 15 miles to bookings these days, although the city centre traffic could sometimes catch him out. He glanced at his watch as he sat at a junction, waiting for the lights to change. Five-thirty.

Damn! He was going to get caught in the rush hour. He reached for his mobile and started dialling as the lights went to green. Playing a strange balancing game he juggled the gear-stick, the phone, the indicators and the steering wheel as he drove on and waited for Harriet to answer. He had nearly given up when the line clicked open and a peevish voice barked, 'Yes?'

'Harriet, Tom,' and when she softened a little he said, 'I hope I caught you before you left home.' She confirmed that he had – just – and he sighed in quiet relief. 'That's good. It's just that I'm running late and I'm getting caught in the traffic. Can we put it back about an hour, please? Will that be a problem?' He could hear Harriet shrug her shoulders on the other end of the line.

'Shouldn't be. Shall I ring and make a booking to be safe?'

'Please,' he said. 'See you later,' and rang off, barely avoiding running into the back of a mini in the process.

Later on he was in a bad mood. The journey home had taken far longer than he had expected and he'd hardly had time to shower, tidy himself up and get out to the restaurant. As it was he was nearly ten minutes late, and he knew how much Harriet hated waiting on her own. He didn't blame her. Restaurants were social places and he always thought there was nothing so sad as someone in a restaurant on their own. He could see her as he arrived. At least she had had the sense to wait at the bar where she was a little less conspicuous. He hurried up to her, apologizing as he air-kissed both cheeks. 'You look nice,' he approved.

She smiled. 'I know,' she said, looking hot and sultry

for an instant before breaking the illusion with a giggle. 'I knew you'd be tired and probably fed up and I thought the least I could do for you was dress up a bit and give you some glam!' She gave him a coquettish glance and added, 'Besides, I might pull!'

He finally smiled back. 'Looking like that, you might just,' he said. 'Come on, let's go straight in – I'm starving.'

'Oh, and another bottle of the Merlot, please.' Tom was feeling mellow but when Harriet's eyebrows went up he had to defend himself. 'Oh come on, Hattie. It's not as if I do this regularly. Besides, you've drunk as much as me and I doubt you'll say no to a glass or two more.' Harriet pushed herself back, feeling comfortably full and couldn't find it in herself to deny him. Somehow the thought of apricot tart with butterscotch ice cream and several glasses more wine seemed very appealing. She drained her glass and put it down in front of her.

'So, Tom, how's it been?' He sighed. She always asked. It was the point of their regular get-togethers, after all, but he always hated the moment when she actually forced him to look back at the previous few weeks.

'OK, I suppose,' he began, but she stopped him with a slightly raised hand and a sharp interruption.

'Ah-ah! We had an agreement,' she said. 'No OKs – nothing is ever OK. It's good or it's bad or you don't care but "OK" doesn't mean anything, so start again.' He knew better than to argue.

'All right then, it's been pretty dire.'

'No bookings?'

'Quite the opposite – I had three last-minute bookings this week. Apparently the Amazing Bongo's got shingles and he's had to cancel all his bookings. There's a whole heap of panicking parents out there running around like headless chickens, all trying to book a late substitute for little Lucia's party. I'm suddenly in demand!'

'Isn't that good?' Harriet asked cautiously. 'I mean, bookings is money, right?'

'Oh, it pays well enough. I won't starve this week, or next. But it's just so...' – he sighed deeply – 'soul destroying, that's what it is. I hate being a clown. I really hate it. But it seems it's all I'm good at. Ironic, isn't it? Big smiley face, but inside...'

Harriet was silent a moment or two, and then said even more cautiously, 'You should come back to church.' Quiet. Gentle. She held her breath.

He sighed again. 'What's the point? God obviously isn't interested in me. Why should I pretend an interest in return?'

'I just think it would do you some good. Meet some people. Sit and relax for an hour. You don't have to listen to anything that's being said – just soak up the atmosphere. I'll come with you if you like.' And he knew then that he would be at the little Methodist chapel on Sunday evening, because Harriet would be with him.

As he shuffled along the pew to sit down he whispered, 'You didn't tell me it was the Covenant Service.'

'Didn't I?' she demurred. 'Well, it doesn't matter does it? You aren't going to listen to anything.'

But he did. All through the service he felt as if he was being watched, which was ridiculous as they were sitting in the back row and there was no one else this far back. There was the frieze though. Unusual for a Methodist church, but it had been a gift in memory of someone. Now the face of Christ, triumphant over death, stared out from the side wall, and Tom felt as if those eyes bored into his soul. Every time he glanced at them they seemed to accuse him, seemed to contrive to look sad and hurt, as if Tom had done something to offend them. When it came to the sermon Harriet was right – he didn't hear a word, but it wasn't because he wasn't interested. He was praying. Well, kind of. He was arguing, he decided. Actually more like ranting. He was silently railing against God, demanding to know why he, God, had condemned him, Tom, to a life and a job that he hated. Why hadn't he rescued him? What did he expect from him? How could he expect him to show any respect when his life was as bad as this? What was he going to do about it? And then he heard the minister reading the words of the covenant prayer.

'Christ has many services to be done: some are easy, others are difficult; some bring honour, others bring reproach; some are suitable to our natural inclinations and material interests, others are contrary to both.' Tell me about it, he thought. He suddenly realized people were standing and he stood with them.

'We're saying this bit,' Harriet hissed, pointing to the prayer in the book, and he started reading it automatically along with everyone else.

'I am no longer my own but yours. Your will, not mine, be done in all things, wherever you may place me, in all that I do and in all that I may endure; when there is work for me and when there is none; when I am troubled and when I am at peace.'

Tom's attention was suddenly on what he was saying, part of his mind openly disbelieving the words, the other listening intently. 'Your will be done when I am valued and when I am disregarded; when I find fulfilment and when it is lacking; when I have all things and when I have nothing.'

It seemed as if every word was burning itself onto his tongue, and yet he kept on saying them. 'I willingly offer all I have and am to serve you, as and where you choose.' He was aware of nothing else, just the sound of his own voice and the words it was speaking.

'Glorious and blessed God, Father, Son and Holy Spirit, you are mine and I am yours. May it be so for ever. Let this covenant now made on earth be fulfilled in heaven.'

He never heard the 'Amen', for he sat down, suddenly drained, suddenly very, very tired. He was aware of Harriet's concerned whispering next to him, and aware that his cheeks were wet, but everything else seemed strangely warm and kind of misty.

He was ten minutes late, again, and he knew Harriet hated waiting alone, but she smiled as he approached her, apologizing as he air-kissed both cheeks.

'You look nice,' she said, and smiled. He contrived to blush which only made her smile all the more, so he took her gallantly by the arm.

'Let's just go eat, shall we?', and she willingly allowed herself to be led into the restaurant. For a couple of hours they sat and ate and drank good wine and laughed a lot until eventually Harriet pushed her dessert plate away from her a little and sighed contentedly.

'Do you know, Tom, it's so good to see you this happy.'

Tom swirled his claret around the glass and smiled back at her. 'Quite a turn-up for the books, isn't it? Me – happy!' He took a swig. 'But it's true. I am happy. And it's all your fault!'

'Why me? I can't claim the credit,' she protested, but he stopped her with a slightly raised hand.

'I only went to that Covenant Service because you asked me. And that was what changed my life,' he said, and she sat back, nodding her understanding. He put the glass back on the table, playing with the stem as he spoke. 'I'd become trapped,' he said. 'I was a clown because . . . well, because that's what I had grown into. But the face was a mask and behind it I was desperately unhappy. I felt resentful that I hadn't amounted to more than a slapstick fool and convinced that I was not fulfilling whatever potential I believed I once had. It's a horrible feeling, being caged. But then I spoke those words. At first I was just saying them because everyone else was but as we went on I began to realize what it was I was saying. And you know what? They really hit home. I mean, really home. I'd been railing against God for such a long time, telling him he owed me and never once stopping to think that it might be me who owed him. After that service I went home and actually opened my

Bible. I hate to think when I last did that but it came open at Jeremiah and the story of the potter and his wheel. I used to do pottery, you know, when I was younger. I used to love putting the clay on the wheel and shaping it, moulding it, forming it into my desired shape. And sometimes it would begin to go wrong a bit so I would bring the clay back to centre and re-shape it – mould it into a new pattern. I realized then that that was what God had been doing with me. He was shaping me, re-shaping me, even if I wasn't aware of it, and if he was waiting, for whatever reasons of his own, well, I had promised to give myself to him regardless of the cost to myself or my circumstance. It was a moment of decision for me but I decided to trust him, because the covenant was a two-way thing – both of us making promises, one to the other.'

He paused, and she was surprised to see a slight glistening in his eyes. 'It was a moment of complete abandon. I offered myself to him without reservation because I felt I had no other option.' He smiled. 'And he didn't let me down.'

Harriet took a swig of her own glass and smiled. She knew what was coming but she never tired of hearing it.

'It was something I remembered a young mother saying to me that made me think. I'd apparently been good for her Down's syndrome son. She'd been grateful but I hadn't really thought about it – until after the service. I began to wonder if there might actually be a purpose to being a clown, whether there might be real potential in the role.' He paused, staring at his glass. 'I started watching the kids while I was performing, really watching them, and I saw something in their faces I'd never seen before. I saw laughter and pleasure, sure, but I also saw wonder and innocence and I finally realized that I might, just, be making a difference.'

'And now you work once a week at the Down's Centre,' she observed. 'Chuckles the Clown – master therapist!'

He snorted. 'I can't claim to have learnt that much,' he said, without any bitterness. 'But I have learnt one important lesson.'

'And what's that?' she asked.

'I've learnt to trust God again,' he said, 'Learnt to trust that he has a purpose for me, that he will mould me and shape me if I let him. And I've learnt one other thing.' He lifted his glass and drained the last of the red wine. 'I've learnt that it's never too late to be re-shaped,' and for a moment she thought his smile looked just like that of Chuckles.

Reflection

I went down to the potter's house, and I saw him working at the wheel. But the pot he was shaping from the clay was marred in his hands; so the potter formed it into another pot, shaping it as seemed best to him.

Jeremiah 18.3–4

Each denomination brings something unique to the rich tapestry of faith. For the Methodist Church it is the Covenant Service. Once a year the church gathers for worship with a sense of solemnity and responsibility unlike any other day, as the service leads them gently but firmly to the saying together of the Covenant Prayer. The words to this prayer are intensely personal, despite being a corporate act, and also intensely challenging. It is not easy to say them and truly mean them, for they at once demand and promise so much.

From our side they demand everything we have and are, but in return God promises to renew his watch over us, and thus the covenant between us is once again affirmed. It is important to remember that this is not a miracle-working prayer, not a question of what God can do for us. It is actually a prayer of abandonment, of total surrender into the care and keeping of God – an act of trust like no other. But it is this trust, which has been repaid so many times and to so many people, that makes the Covenant Service such a potentially powerful and moving occasion. Over the years many people have found the words of this prayer have spoken to them in a personal and powerful way, discovering afresh what it is to give oneself wholly to God and simply to trust in him. We do well to read the words of Jeremiah occasionally and recall that placing ourselves into God's hands and allowing him to shape and to mould us is at the very heart of our faith.

Learning to love

There is blood. There are tears. The sound of crying, panting, exhaustion and elation. She lies on the bed, sweat-drenched, eyes closed, her ripped flesh bloody in the private places. It hurts. Oh, it hurts where the not-so-tiny head tore her apart emerging into the world, blood-stained and traumatized. Feet clasped together, upside down, bottom slapped until the pain forces sharp gasps of air into his lungs. And then arms reaching eagerly for him, tenderly, (oh so tenderly), clasping his tiny form to her breast. She softly strokes away the blood, cleaning the mess from his hair, whispering words that have no meaning, washing his face with her tears. He was warm and safe in the darkness, wrapped in the life-giving fluid, only to be forced through the pain into the bright, hostile world outside. His heart beats fast, his newborn mind unable to grasp the significance of the change. And it is only her warmth that eases him, only her love so palpably given that assures him. A concept grasped but not understood. Today love is a warm breast and security, his only comfort in a hostile world.

In darkness he waited, preparing for the adventure – the die cast, the decision made. More blood. More tears. More pain as she lies in the straw, pushing her God unknowing into the world. And amid the torn flesh and afterbirth, in pain and confusion, omnipotence is exchanged for innocence as he enters the world like any other, ignorant of everything but hunger and need and fear. But she reaches for him, clasping him to her sweat-soaked breast. Softly stroking away the blood she whispers words with no meaning, washes his face with her tears. And in the darkness of the animal stall, fragile and dependent, the God of Love is taught love by the woman who gives him life. And it begins ...

There is blood. There are tears. Pain and shame mingled together. Blood from the nose where the fist connected. Tears of surprise more than pain and tears of shame – a mother's tongue can scold as sharply as fists, and the pain lasts longer, cuts deeper. Even as she tends the wound she lashes with words, tenderness and anger coexisting, focusing on the boy. Head hung, tears squeezing their way out where the words sting. He does not try to explain, does not make excuses. It made sense at the time. It seemed natural, even sensible, and he did not think of the consequences. Until now. And so he stands, accepting what comes. At an instinctive level he understands that his mother's anger is more to do with what might have happened than the physical harm he has actually suffered. But something has changed. Her love is no longer just the warm, comfortable security of his infancy. It is a hard-edged force, at once pragmatic and sacrificial – silk with an edge. It is still warm. It is still secure. But there is steel within it.

*

In the Temple they find him, almost the last place they could think of. More in desperation than hope. They made assumptions. They will not do so again. Not your average runaway this, trawling the souks and the markets. That would have been easy. But to find him here, in the Temple, debating theology with the teachers. Not average at all. Nor repentant ('Did you not know?'). But surprised. Surprised at his mother's words. Surprised at her anger. Surprised at her tears. Surprised at the punishment. Today the God of Love is learning about fear and worry and desperate searching. Learning that love is not only about laughter and friendship and warmth and security, but about steel and about edge. And for reasons he does not yet understand that worries him.

It is their wedding day and he waits nervously by the altar, seeking that first glimpse of silk and veil. She walks slowly towards him, a known mystery, and their eyes meet as before, and yet for the first time. Side by side they stand. Rings are given, vows taken, a kiss exchanged, and their lives are forever joined. Smiles and tears in the ritual of union. One man and one woman, bound in flesh and blood, heart and mind, life and soul. If love were an ocean they would talk of drowning in its depths, but for this day they are content to bathe in its shallows, knowing there is time to explore its reaches in the days and years to come. This day is sufficient. Today love is a promise, a commitment, a covenant – manifest in smiles and hands entwined, witnessed by friends and family, legalized by the pen. Love looks to the future, even as it overwhelms the present.

*

At a wedding in Cana he sits and watches the celebrations, made all the merrier by water turned into wine. Somehow he knows he will never experience such a day for himself, knows his path is elsewhere. But he watches and learns. The newly-wed couple talk quietly, no overt signs of affection, but then this was not essentially their choice. If not arranged, then at least encouraged. Family, always family. Yet he can see the potential between them, the promise of love no matter what may come, and the commitment to the unknown future. And it is firing ideas for his teaching. A metaphor for the promise he will make, the commitment he knows he will give. Amid the laughter of celebration the God of Love hears the echo of his covenant, begins to understand the nature of his love. Begins to see where it might lead...

It has been hard work these last few months and he is tired. So many demands, so little time. And she has been hurt so. First there was joy, excitement at the news. And then happy hours discussing names and colour schemes. Until the day she lost the child, a boy as it happened. A stumble on the stairs, pain within and an ambulance journey to more pain. He came as soon as he heard, the shaking heads of doctors waiting for him, to sit and hold her hand and share the pain. And her healing has taken time. He felt it, too, but she killed the child. It was her feet that tripped, her body that did not cushion him, that ejected him too soon, and she has assumed the guilt, assumed the blame. Healing is not always physical and he has learnt much about wholeness and self-esteem and acceptance. Learnt it as he has taught it. At first their promise was a warm, happy excitement. Love was a physical thing, finding fulfilment in her conception. But he has grown. He has learnt the lesson his mother taught, that love is not only about receiving, but about giving. He has given her of himself and her healing is the result. Now their love is something else. A promise, yes. A commitment, yes. But it has a depth and a resonance that they never imagined. And all because he learnt to give.

He is tired, but then it has been hard. So many demands, so little time. The first flush of excitement carried him along to begin with. But reality is hard. Soon they press round him. Calling. Pleading. Touching. First he was a teacher. Now he is a healer. Daily they come – the crippled, the blind, the diseased, the disturbed. Demanding. Begging. But he has time for them all. He makes the time. He has learnt about wholeness and acceptance, learnt that healing is only sometimes a physical process. He has learnt, too, that it is in the giving of himself that his love finds its true expression. And he is just beginning to understand how much he will have to give. Amid the crowds and the adulation the God of Love feels very alone, as he gives his love to anyone who needs it.

He is numb, completely numb – the mind's defence against the doctor's sentence. Three months. Maybe six. More with chemotherapy, if he thinks the price is worth paying. Of course he need not decide now. Take some time. But not too much. There is no more potential. The future folded in an instant, swallowing hopes and dreams and ambitions. She feels the unfairness most. He is too young. They were going to do things together. They had their whole lives to live. And now the doctor has drawn a line across their path – this far, but beyond you walk alone. And she does not know what to feel, how to react. Her love, which has wrapped him round in the blossom and bloom of her promise, is suddenly a cold, blue light. Sharp and piercing. Joy turned to bitter pain. They have fought this moment. Hoped. Prayed. Clung to a future of remission. But there comes a moment of absolute knowledge, and with it resolution. The blue light gives her strength as she resolves in her love to carry him these last few months. There will be time for grief later, when she is alone. But for now her love is a strength she never knew, a rock upon which to anchor his decline. She will survive. She will see him through. Her promise has just called its price and she finds she has the strength to pay it. Love is not only a commitment. Today love is both a source of power and a terrible burden.

He is numb. Completely numb. The tranquillity of the garden has focused his mind, clarified the future, and its painful inevitability has hit him like a rock. He is too young. There is so much to do, so much potential to be realized, so much living to be done. But a line has been drawn and if he chooses to accept it the cold certainty of the end will swallow him within hours. He has fought this moment. Hoped. Prayed even. Clung to a different future. But there comes a moment of absolute knowledge, and with it resolution. He has learnt so much about the nature of love, has put so much of it into practice. But in the garden this evening he is discovering the cold, blue light, and with it a source of power. Tonight the God of Love accepts that the promise has become a burden and finds he has the strength to carry it. Beneath the olive trees he is coming to understand that love has never cost so much. Nor ever will.

He is dying. They said three months, maybe six. He has gone five, saying no to chemotherapy. When it can't change the outcome why spoil what you have left? He has been active and they have *lived* these last few months. Really lived. But the end has come and he lies on the bed, a broken shell. There is pain, great pain, and though he has fought for life now he longs for the end, for the doors to close. Or maybe open. He's not sure which. She sits in vigil by his bed, as she has for three days now, snatching sleep in the chair whenever he was quiet. She has held him and wiped him and watched him suffer, and though she cannot imagine the world without him she, too, wants an end. The promise become burden has finally become a privilege as she finds her true self in service to him. But she is tired, as is he, and part of her will welcome the finish. It comes in the night. There is no drama, little to mark the passage from life to death. He is with her and then he is gone, and she knows it.

The budding promise of her love has blossomed and bloomed in the caring and the sharing of their lives, but now, when some might expect it to fade, she finds it overwhelming her. The months of strength and coping are suddenly gone and her grief can find its release. And so the tears come, washing his lifeless face, washing her soul. In the months to come she will rebuild her life, alone, but the love they shared will have borne fruit. She will be stronger. She will be more whole. She will be a source of strength to others and a beacon in the darkness of life. She will survive. She will shine. And all because she learnt to love.

He is dying. The nails have ripped his flesh, torn his sinews, pinned him to the cross and he is suffocating. It has come too soon, only hours since the garden. And it has been all he feared. And more. His back is raw where the lead weights in the whip have torn strips from his skin. His ribs are bruised and swollen from the beating. His blood trickles down his face where the thorns have been pushed into his head. And the nails grind against his nerves, hot agony with every movement, every breath.

He has fought this. Hoped and prayed against it, finally embraced it. It has to be done. It must be. But somehow he thought it would be different, more certain. He has followed his Father's will for three years, gradually grasping what the price would be, but now, at the end, why does he feel so alone? Where is the confirmation that he is right, that he has done the right thing? Where is the sign? Where is the miracle? Where is anything at all? The promise become burden has become unbearable and now he longs for the end. Or will it be a beginning? He's not so sure any more. All he knows is that it is finished and that he is alone. Utterly alone. And then he is gone.

On a cross on a hill the God of Love dies in agony. It began with blood and tears, and so it ends. In between he has learnt love at his mother's breast and seen it harden in her frightened anger. He has understood love to be a promise, a commitment and a demand, requiring him to give and give and give of himself, no matter what the cost. He has seen it become a burden and in the blue light of understanding has embraced it as his destiny. Today the God of Love has paid the ultimate price for people who will never understand, who will not want to know. It has cost him dear, but the love he has shared with so many will bear fruit. In three days' time he will be stronger. He will be completely whole. He will be a source of strength to others and a beacon in the darkness of life. He will survive. He will shine. And others will live. And all because the God of Love learnt to love.

Reflection

One of the teachers of the law came and heard them debating. Noticing that Jesus had given them a good answer, he asked him, 'Of all the commandments, which is the most important?'

'The most important one,' answered Jesus, 'is this: "Hear, O Israel, the Lord our God, the Lord is one. Love the Lord your God with all your heart and with all your soul and with all your mind and with all your strength." The second is this: "Love your neighbour as yourself." There is no commandment greater than these.'

Mark 12.28–31

If I have to sum up the essence of my Christian faith in one word that word would be 'love'. The limitations of the English language frustrate me here, for we have only the single word to describe a concept so deep, so wonderful, so terrifying and so utterly essential to all that we are and can become as human beings. And nowhere do we see love more powerfully and more beautifully expressed than in the life of Jesus. It never ceases to amaze me that at the heart of our faith is an act of such utter barbarity as the crucifixion. I understand why we do not like to look too closely. Yet it is here, within the very heart of humankind's most brutal disrespect for life, that love takes wing and reveals itself in all its incandescent wonder.

From time to time I have heard people complain that they cannot relate to Jesus, cannot take him seriously precisely because he was the Son of God. How can he understand what their lives are like? How can he understand their pain, their confusion, their frustrations? My answer is always the same. I have never been one to see Jesus as a benign, saint-like man sailing serenely through life. My Christ was fully human and had to learn everything the hard way – just as I have done – and I suspect it was a real struggle for him. If we truly look at his life we can see so many parallels with our own, no matter who we are or what we have experienced. Ultimately that is what makes the Christian faith so utterly compelling; we can never accuse God of not understanding us because in almost every situation he has truly 'been there, done that' before us.

The Bible teaches us that we reflect the image of God.

Because of Jesus I know that whatever the world throws at me I can trust my life to God for the very simple reason that he knows what it is like to live. When he decided to enter this world for himself he chose to explore that image in all its human frailty as well as its beauty – he learnt like I did – and in so doing made himself small in order to get really close to his creation. For me God's willingness to risk himself in that way is what makes Christianity so unique, and ironically it is what gives it its true strength. Jesus shows us how hard it can be to live, but he also shows us how the human life can be something truly wonderful when lived in communion with God.

I find that whenever life seems too demanding, whenever the demands of love seem too great, I have only to look again at the life of Christ for everything to fall into its proper perspective.

Jesus is a truth that never fails to inspire me.